The Healing Experience

*What People Are Saying
About Ricardo F. Dorcean's*

The Healing Experience

"As an Inner Healing Minister with Restoring the Foundations, International I was honored to be one of the first to read this exceptionally written book. *The Healing Experience* will challenge you not to live in bondage, pain and woundedness all your life but to thirst for the healing that Father God wants for each of his children. *The Healing Experience* will take you on a journey of self-inventory, as well as challenge you to take a look at how you are really dealing with life challenges, life's ups and downs in every relationship in your life.
It will move you to another level of freedom and give you a fresh new outlook on your past and move you into your future. It is Biblically sound and practical and worth your time to really set aside time to spend with God while not only reading *The Healing Experience* but meditating on it and allowing God to minister to your heart with every page that you read. *The Healing Experience* will help you see that healing is one of the most precious gifts Father God has given us His precious children and there is no shame in running to receive Life Changing and Life Giving Healing Ministry."

Pastor Pauline Ezell
Restoring the Foundations Minister

I love the concept and the creativity of how Pastor Ricardo Dorcean strategically weaves the words of this book together. He takes time to build a 21st century case study if you will, *on THE HEALING EXPERIENCE*. As believers it starts with a true understanding and comprehension of the truth as we see it via our manuscript for life, The Bible. Then, as life happens we must be prepared to overcome all of our crazy obstacles and heal. Of course, it's many times easier said than done. However, I believe if you're looking for concrete evidence on what God can do to help create your own healing experience, this book does just that. Be prepared to be challenged in your thoughts and actions as you prepare for your very own Healing Experience.

Dwann Holmes
Lead Pastor - Global Prophetic Life Training and Worship Embassy
Founder - The Global Institute of Church & Marketplace Prophets

---

At the lowest point in my life God sent me, *"The Healing Experience"* to lead me into the promises of wholeness as my pain ravished my hopes of ever experiencing divine healing. Ricardo F. Dorcean's masterpiece gently commanded me to show God where it hurts while encouraging me to see the victory I have in being vulnerable with my Father. I hungrily devoured the words flowing off the pages as healing poured into my hurting soul. This divine work will help countless sons and daughters experience God's healing in every area of their lives...

Dr. YaQuanda McCall, founder
I Speak Life Global Min. Inc.
5am Prayer International SHiFT

In his up-to-the-minute address of the ubiquitous nature of human suffering and pain, Dorcean brilliantly examines the multifaceted aspects of life in the raw—in its organic and unadorned form. Dorcean deliberately dances with the jagged and dissonant sounds of human suffering while offering the "ageless" antidote of God's word. *The Healing Experience* is a must have in the age of the disconsolate.

Kurt S. Clark, DMin.
Pastor of Sardis MBC
Birmingham, AL

The Healing Experience is exactly what the title asserts. As a survivor of various traumas and as one who has been seeking the "Actual thing" that heals the soul and not merely covers up emotional and physical pain, Pastor Dorcean has written the "aha" moment. God wants us to experience healing that shifts us from hurt to a level of healing that can be maintained beyond the moment of its manifestation". Dorcean carefully and thoughtfully leads the seeker through tangible steps that go beyond the habit of some to practice applying scripture without addressing the psychological suffering, physical pain and persistent hope one has in the power to heal. Ricardo has managed to nuance this work in an authentic nonjudgmental way that encourages one to confidently trust his discernment and methodology -- Caring, Careful, Honest and Beneficial to the body and the soul.

Marquita Carmichael, DMin
Assistant Director of Religious
Life & Our Serenity Group, LLC. CEO

This is a very beautiful read, delicately strung together to serve its purpose of guidance through the very hectic process of healing and recovery. The author is very delicate with his words, fostering a deep sense of spiritual awareness in the reader. He keeps the reader grounded at every single point of the journey, steady reminding us, that the focus and pivotal point in this journey of healing, is always God, whichever way the road leads, it will always lead one back to God, who is willing and able to deliver us from life's struggles and unending drama—as long as we are willing to tap into that abundant grace.

This was a spirit lifting read, and I definitely recommend, for anyone in search or longing for true peace, stability and wholesome existence.

Editorial Review
Maximized Productions, LLC.

The Healing Experience

Ricardo F. Dorcean

Foreword by Bishop Joseph W. Walker III

The Healing Experience copyright © 2021 by Ricardo F. Dorcean

All rights reserved. No part of this publication may be reproduced, stored in a retrieval system, or transmitted in any form by any means, electronic, mechanical, photocopy, recording, or otherwise, without the prior permission of the publisher, except as provided for by USA copyright law.

ISBN: 978-1-7352672-5-8

Published by Maximized Productions, LLC.

UPH Publishing Div.

6715 Suitland Rd. – Morningside, MD 20746

www.maximizedproductions.com

Cover Design: Maximized Productions, LLC.

UPH Pub. Div.

Book Design by Dawn M. Harvey

Please direct your inquiries to the address above or visit:

Phone: 423-292-0836

Email:Ricardo@dorceanenterprises.com

RicardoDorcean (Facebook, Twitter, Instagram)

Register for The Healing Experience Program at https://www.kissfromheaven.life/

PRINTED IN THE UNITED STATES OF AMERICA

3 John 1:2

"Beloved, I pray that you may prosper in all things and be in health, just as your soul prospers."

DEDICATION

This book is dedicated to countless, courageous individuals who have experienced or may be experiencing hurt, but continues to embrace opportunities to do the healing work that helps bring healing and wholeness into their lives.

Secondly, this book is dedicated to the Pastors, Spiritual counselors, Inner Healing Ministers, and Mental Health Professionals who sacrificially step into the spaces of people's sufferings to serve as safe support systems in order to help shift individuals towards the successful state of becoming the best version of themselves.

Most importantly, this book is dedicated to my wife, Chaka, who is the love of my life and my best friend. Babe, God used you to open my eyes and enlighten my understanding to the need for this kind of healing experience in the church and in our world at large. Thank you for walking with me in our own personal healing experience and for walking with me in this journey of providing safe spaces and serving as strong support systems for those who seek and are in need of God's healing experiences for their lives.

Foreword by Bishop Joseph Warren Walker, III

Pain is one of the inevitable realities of life. Billions of dollars are spent in the pharmaceutical industry in an attempt to medicate and mitigate its effect on our lives. Very few of us are gluttons for pain and often find ourselves doing everything we can to avoid it. What we all know is that no matter how we attempt to avoid it, pain is an equal opportunity employer. In fact, there are so many dimensions of pain that we often find ourselves going from one traumatic experience to another. Perhaps this is what Jesus assured us would occur in John 16:33. "These things I have spoken to you, that in Me you may have peace. In the world you will have tribulation, but be of good cheer, I've already overcome the world."

Owning our pain and having the courage to work through it toward a solution is what this powerful book is about. Ricardo Dorcean has given us a road map toward healing. His willingness to be transparent lends itself to the empathy that permeates each page. I have found it difficult to receive instruction from people who have not lived the experiences they share with others. It is very clear that he has lived the healing experience and we are benefactors of the blessings he learned from them.

This book is not for the faint at heart. It is designed for those who are willing to take the deep dive toward healing and deliverance. When we make the decision to be whole, we must be willing to do what God requires even if it stretches us. This book gives biblical insight and practical steps to help us walk through the healing experience. It becomes clear early on that healing is available for all who want it. This is more than a great book, it's a manual full of instructions that I'm confident will be an asset to all who read it.

INTRODUCTION

There they were sitting at the kitchen table. The epitome of a love story. Jacob and Rachel provided the picture-perfect portrait of a life filled with happiness and wholeness. They were the television sitcom version of Phil and Vivian Banks from The Fresh Prince of Bel-air or Carl and Harriet Winslow from Family Matters. They lived in a nice big house and drove nice cars. They were employed by a very successful company. They were engaged in their community and in the activities and lives of their children. They were entrusted with and effective in various leadership responsibilities as members of their local church. Whether it was their picture-perfect marriage, their picture-perfect family or their overall picture-perfect lives, these two seemed to have it all together. With this couple, it just seemed like regardless of what life threw their way, they continued to smile, remained strong and lived successful lives. They were the couple that everyone wanted to be, but didn't actually think was possible to become. They were Jacob and Rachel. However, on this day, they had a look on their faces that was unfamiliar to me and I would imagine, unfamiliar to anyone who experienced their lives from an outsider's perspective. From the vantage point of many who witnessed their togetherness and many who simply got wind of it, Jacob and Rachel were the ideal couple. If one's marriage, one's family, one's career or one's life could mirror the happiness that was put on display for public consumption, then the obvious conclusion would be complete success, or would it? You see, while their public presentation provided the perception that would result in much popularity and power and prestige and prominence, there was another presentation that was waiting for the opportunity to be propelled beyond the private places of Jacob and Rachel's lives. This presentation was not fueled by Jacob and Rachel's position or their prosperity. It was not fueled by their prestige or prominence within society. This presentation that was planted deep within them was being fueled by their painful experiences. This presentation was hidden within a heart that housed a lot of hurt. Within their hearts, they housed the hurt of traumatic experiences that stemmed from their childhood. Their experiences included domestic abuse, substance abuse, family secrets, divorce and much more. While these experiences were a part of their history, on that day, it became clear that the hurts from their history was still creating hang ups in their current reality. What many on the outside didn't know, was that this picture-perfect portrait was on the verge of being completely dismantled and destroyed. Divorce was imminent. The family was struggling to survive. Employment was about to be taken away. Their picture-perfect world was in crisis and crumbling fast. This was Jacob and Rachel's experience and it was an experience that they were able to consistently escape and evade with their presentation of a picture-perfect life. The more they operated as the persons in the picture they presented, the more oppressive their pain had the potential to become in their lives. It was at that moment that God birthed the revelation that would begin to remedy what was about to ruin their lives. It became clear to me that Jacob and Rachel were in need of The Healing Experience. There has to be an experience of healing to handle the hurts that have the potential to hinder our wholeness. What I have discovered is, this experience of healing has already been factored into the fruit of the Power of The Gospel and Grace that Jesus has made available and accessible to us. This is why I love God so much. God loves us enough not to leave us handcuffed or handicapped by the inevitable experiences of hurt, but rather, we are given access to the healing experience that is authorized by Heaven. This is what Jacob and Rachel discovered. And like them, all of us have moments and measures of hurt that may be requesting and even requiring healing experiences. Whether you are the star of your high school football team, the CEO of your company, The President of your country, or like me, ministers of the Gospel of Jesus Christ, you have either experienced or will experience hurt that needs healing experiences. You see, I personally understand the story of Jacob and Rachel. Even as ministers of the Gospel of Jesus Christ, the marriage that my wife Chaka and I are currently growing and thriving in is a by-product of God's healing experiences in our lives. As a matter of fact, while going through our hurtful experiences, God took us through a process of healing that has been continually consistent in cultivating and sustaining healing and wholeness in our lives. Throughout this book, you will be introduced to and walked through this particular process of healing that God used to bring healing into my life and the life of many others. As you take the journey through this book with me, it is my prayer and my faith-filled projection that God will help you matriculate through a variety of moments and measures of The Healing Experience that you may need to begin living your best life. Get Ready for The Healing Experience.

TABLE OF CONTENTS

SHOW ME WHERE IT HURTS 22

FINDING VICTORY IN VULNERALBILITY 62

MORE LEVELS OF LIFE TO LIVE 86

THERE IS DELIVERANCE IN DISCONNECTING 109

LIVING THE HEALED LIFE 129

How Do I Use My Journal Pages?

It is Ricardo's hope that as he shares his lessons with you, that you too will pen the lessons you learn while reading this book. Also, feel free to write your memories, goals and dreams on your journal pages.

CHAPTER ONE

SHOW ME WHERE IT HURTS

If you are reading this book, or at the least, if you are alive today, you have either experienced hurt, you are currently experiencing hurt or you are on your way to experiencing some measure of hurt. While these experiences are inevitable and imminent, God has a healing experience for our lives that will counter the hurtful experiences of our lives. This healing experience has a process that we will explore and engage throughout this book. The first part of the healing experience process is the work of showing God the areas of our lives that are hurting. If we are serious about experiencing healing that Heaven makes available and accessible to us, there has to be a level of maturity within our relationship with God that empowers us to operate with a level of trust in God that will at least show God where we are hurting.

This level of trust is something that is natural to most children. If you are a parent or if you have ever been around a child who has experienced an injury or a "boo-boo," one of the first things they will do is communicate that they are in pain and with that communication, they will also point to the area that is hurting them. Without even thinking about it, children will share the hurt because they operate with a level of trust that their parents care and will try to do whatever they

The Healing Experience

possibly can do to help make them feel better. Children trust that if they can just show where it hurts, their parents can help make it better or at the least, provide that magical kiss that somehow gives them power to deal with the pain. You see, that's the kind of relationship that God desires to have with us and that's the kind of relationship that the healing experience will demand of us. God desires and healing demands a relationship of total and complete trust in God, the kind of trust that allows us to show Him where we hurt. That trust is not something that we can just declare, but it must become something that we demonstrate. It must be exemplified and when it comes to experiencing Healing from God, our trust in God must be exemplified in our willingness to do the work of transparency and vulnerability with God. It is our ability and our actions of showing God where we hurt that begins the application of the healing that God will customize for our particular experiences. Healing will never truly happen for us until we are able and willing to show God where we are experiencing hurt in our lives. Oftentimes, the natural response and rationale to handling hurt is to hide the hurt in an attempt to minimize the measure of hurt we may be experiencing. In other words, if we can just conceal it, we can control it from causing even more calamity in our lives. Here is the rationale: If I hide it, then at least, I won't have to deal with the opinionated observations and condemnatory commentary of those who witnessed and are witnessing my wounds. If I can just hide it, at least, I won't get judged. By concealing my hurt, I can at least ensure that my wounds won't be used as a weapon against me. Then there are those who conceal their hurts because they don't want to be viewed as wounded and weak. Regardless of the rationale, at the crux of the concealment is a spirit of control which gains access to us by the spirit of fear that begins to operate once doors are opened by the hurts we experience. To combat this and counter this demonic strategy of hiding

The Healing Experience

our hurts, God gives us the strength and the strategy to show Him our hurts. The heart of healing that Heaven gives us access to calls for a resistance against the temptation to hide our hurts. While it may feel natural and while it may seem reasonable to shield our hurts, and while there are times, it may be the responsible response to our hurts, when it comes to The Healing Experience, we must be willing to defy the rationales and reasons that we have restricted people to and simply trust God enough to show God where we hurt.

Now, while it may sound like a simple process, we recognize that what often is pictured in simplicity is planted in complexity. When it comes to our hurts, the reality is, while God wants us to show Him where the hurts are in our lives, the reality is we often end up trying to deal with the hurt on our own or in our own way without ever taking the time to show God where we hurt. Part of the reasons we do that is because our humanity falls victim to the powerful influence of the spirit of fear and control. As a result, we take it upon ourselves to confront and cope with the hurts that we have experienced or continue to experience and we often end up omitting the significance of God's power to heal, in the process of trying to handle our hurts. Much of what we see in the world and in the church as it relates to hurt and healing are incomplete results or underdeveloped results of healing, trying to handle various experiences with hurt. What I am learning like many before me have learned and many are learning today is, if we are serious about experiencing true and lasting healing, we must approach the pursuit of healing with a strategy that prioritizes transparency so that the solutions aren't temporary.

You see without transparency, there can be no real transformative testimonies of healing in our lives. When we look at the United States of America, particularly in light of all of the racial resistance and unrest, what we are witnessing are the results of a country that has

The Healing Experience

experienced incomplete and underdeveloped results of healing that is now trying to handle various experiences with racial hurt, that continues to hover in the hidden halls of not only this country's history, but even in this country's present-day reality. Throughout history, the agenda and approach has seemingly been to conceal in order to control the narrative, instead of confronting in order to correct the navigation so that it leads to sincere and strategic healing within the country. As a result, instead of initiating important and insightful conversations, we indulge in the ignorance of conducts that perpetuate the hurt and prolong the experience of healing that is needed in this country. Again, the healing experience, whether it is singular or societal, will require transparency and without a truthful measure of transparency, we will always struggle to transition this country into the experiences of transformative testimonies of healing. Now the key to our transparency being effective in helping us heal is to make sure that those whom we allow to share in our transparency must be able to love us in our truth. If people can't love us in our truth, how can we expect them to lead us to any kind of transformative healing? You see, part of the reason why racial hurt continues to dominate the fabric of the United States is because African Americans and other minorities, who have been sharing transparency with the hopes that it will help transition this country into transformative testimonies of healing, continue to be tackled by thoughts and tenets that struggle to love us in our truth. On the flipside, if America is truly interested in having a healing experience, America is blessed to have ethnic minority citizens who have been and are continuously willing to love those who have benefited and continue to benefit from systems that perpetuate the racial hurt that continues to be experienced in this country. America has citizens who will love her in all of her truth. The key is, there must be a willingness to engage transparently from all angles and there must

The Healing Experience

be a willingness to love those who share in the truth of their transparency. Because this level of transparency within the context of human experiences, it is often difficult to execute for various reasons. I want to offer the initial groundwork to help develop the practice of the kind of transparency that will be effective in helping manifest the healing experience. If the human context is too overwhelming to do the work of transparency, then we ought to allow our relationship with God to be the initial platform where we are willing to be transparent with our hurts. When we consider that Our Heavenly Father, in His Omniscience, already has the fullness of complete knowledge concerning all of existence throughout the entirety of eternity, then it is safe to suggest that God already knows our truths before we are even aware of them and He chooses to love us in spite of them. Who better to trust with our transparency, than the God who loves us perfectly? If you are experiencing hurt and you are hiding it because you don't feel you can trust anyone to be able to handle your transparency, I want to encourage you to test God with your transparency. This, however, will require a level of humility that would empower us to release control to God, so that healing can be experienced. When real healing is the goal, there will eventually come the realization, that regardless of what our methods of coping and healing may be, regardless of who we invite to address the afflictions that have caused us harm, true healing only transfers into our lives when we can humble ourselves enough to be transparent with God. You see, when the hurt may have been addressed, the impact and infection will eventually invade our lives until we make a decision to trust God enough to be vulnerable and transparent with our hurts. Now, many people don't understand the need to show God where it hurts because God, in His omniscience and omnipresence, God in His infinite knowledge and ever-present nature should know exactly where my hurts exist. While that is true, God's

The Healing Experience

nature also resists the action of invasion and simply waits for the invitation. We have to invite God into our hurts because God will only heal, not what we conceal, but what we're willing to reveal. Here is a powerful truth about God and our hurts: God is never disinterested or dismissive about our hurts, but rather, He has a deep desire to demonstrate His love for us by being present in the places where pain is prevailing in our lives. The heart of God, The Father, is to empower us with the healing experience that we need to authentically have victory over the hurts we have experienced in our lives. It becomes our responsibility to tap into our faith capacity and trust God enough to show God where it hurts.

An example of this part of the healing experience is found in the life experience of two sisters, Mary and Martha. These two sisters experienced a devastating level of hurt that is recorded for us in the Gospel of John. The following is the scriptural record of this particularly heartbreaking experience:

> *1 A man named Lazarus, who lived in Bethany, became sick. Bethany was the town where Mary and her sister Martha lived. (2 This Mary was the one who poured the perfume on the Lord's feet and wiped them with her hair; it was her brother Lazarus who was sick.) 3 The sisters sent Jesus a message: "Lord, your dear friend is sick." 17 When Jesus arrived, he found that Lazarus had been buried four days before. 18 Bethany was less than two miles from Jerusalem, 19 and many Judeans had come to see Martha and Mary to comfort them about their brother's death. 20 When Martha heard that Jesus was coming, she went out to meet him,*

The Healing Experience

but Mary stayed in the house. 21 Martha said to Jesus, "If you had been here, Lord, my brother would not have died! 28 After Martha said this, she went back and called her sister Mary privately. "The Teacher is here," she told her, "and is asking for you." 29 When Mary heard this, she got up and hurried out to meet him. (30 Jesus had not yet arrived in the village, but was still in the place where Martha had met him.) 31 The people who were in the house with Mary comforting her followed her when they saw her get up and hurry out. They thought that she was going to the grave to weep there. 32 Mary arrived where Jesus was, and as soon as she saw him, she fell at his feet. "Lord," *she said,* "if you had been here, my brother would not have died!" *33 Jesus saw her weeping, and he saw how the people with her were weeping also; his heart was touched, and he was deeply moved. 34* "Where have you buried him?" *he asked them.* "Come and see, Lord," *they answered. (John 11:1-3, 17-21, 28-34 Good News Translation)*

In this life experience, we find an extreme level of hurt being experienced by Martha and Mary. They are experiencing the pain and suffering of losing their brother Lazarus, whom they loved. After he dies, they go through the process of having his funeral and then burying him. What has happened from a symbolic perspective, is they have now buried the thing that resulted in their hurt. Lazarus is not simply their brother, but Lazarus in his death represents the symbol of their hurt. The death of their brother hurt them and they bury it. Now, if you consider the symbolism from a life application perspective, Mary and Martha's response to their hurt is very similar to the

The Healing Experience

responses that many people have had and continue to have as it relates to the personal hurts of life. People will often bury what hurts them. Whether it's the hurt of losing a loved one to death, the hurt of divorce, the hurt of being violated and victimized, the hurt of being judged or discriminated against, the proclivity within our humanity is to simply bury the hurt and try to move on with life.

This concept of burying the hurt and moving on from the hurt is found in verse 17 of the scripture reference. We see that four days after burying their brother, or burying their hurt, Jesus shows up. The time frame suggests that the process of death is definite and complete. They are now going to try to move on from it. They are going to try and cope with the death of their brother. While trying to accept this new reality of life without their brother, Jesus enters the scene and the moment they encounter Jesus, they began to express emotions of anger and disappointment that were presented in the form of blame directed at Jesus. It is quite interesting that even though they have already buried their brother and were trying to move on from it, the hurt was still raw and relevant to their reality. Even though they buried their brother, who again symbolizes the hurt that they were experiencing, the hurt had already impacted and infected them internally. The evidence of this is found in their attitude of blame towards Jesus. Here is the lesson that their initial interaction with Jesus reveals: Burying our hurts will not release us from being bound to our hurts. They were bound by it and now what they thought had been addressed, had now manifested in their attitude towards Jesus.

Let's consider this lesson in our personal lives. How many times do we try to move on from situations that have hurt us, only to discover that, the hurt we thought we had handled, was simply hiding in a holding cell within our hearts and as long as the hurt is hidden, healing is held hostage. You see, oftentimes, hurts are insulated

The Healing Experience

internally and whenever the hurt is insulated, the heart will get infected and the problem with an infected heart is that the infection is never detected until it is being demonstrated. You don't realize your heart has been infected by the hurt until it shows up in the symptoms of attitudes and behaviors. This is part of what America faces as a nation. Some of the responses that seem angry and counterproductive to healing are the results of the infected hearts of a community that has been inhibited by the racial injustices that are insulated within the heart of this country. While we have attempted to move on, we have only accommodated the actualization of the infection. I can't emphasize enough the essentiality of dealing with the hurts that often remain insulated within us.

Let me paint this picture from my personal perspective. When my wife and I got married, we married each other knowing that we both had deep and damaging details that were a part of our story. The problem that was later revealed was that the issues never went through a thorough or complete healing experience. We discovered that many of the issues that we thought we were healed from were actually insulated within us. It wasn't until later on in our marriage did we gain the understanding, that many of our marital issues were simply the infection of insulation. We began demonstrating behaviors in our marriage that we didn't realize were directly connected to or related to issues that we experienced in our history, as early as our childhood. All of a sudden, both minor and major issues began to arise in our marriage because insulated issues were being left unaddressed. We had issues as minor as arguments that centered on our particular preferences in folding clothes and as major as infidelity. I remember after doing laundry one day, we got into an argument because my clothes weren't folded the way Chaka likes them to be folded. Chaka was adamant about the clothes being folded her way and I stood my

The Healing Experience

ground as it related to how I wanted to fold my clothes. Eventually, I began folding my clothes her way, but unfortunately, that minor disagreement, among others, added to the hurtful experiences that engulfed our marriage.

The most devastating experience in our marriage was my decision to engage in infidelity. This was the most troubling, trifling and traumatic test that I inflicted on my wife and our marriage. Eventually, what I discovered was all of our issues, both minor and major, were behaviors that demonstrated and denoted the infection of our hearts due to the internal insulation of issues. My wife has a saying that perfectly describes what we experienced. She would say, "Anything unaddressed will manifest!" For us, things that were left unaddressed from as far back as childhood to even issues left unaddressed through the early years of our marriage began to manifest itself. It was at this point that we decided to begin the process of addressing our hurts. Up until this moment, we were burying every hurtful experience. We would shut down, suck it up and try to move on, not realizing we were setting ourselves up to live in a sustained state of suffering. We were in desperate need of a healing experience.

Similar to the negative behavioral responses we gave to each other in our marriage, Mary and Martha negatively behaved and responded to Jesus. In the life of experience of Mary and Martha, when the sisters responded to Jesus showing up in their lives, what is clear is that their responses were symptoms of the infection of their heart caused by the hurt of losing their brother. They were clearly upset that their brother died and what intensified their anger was the fact that Jesus took so long to show up. In response to their attitude, Jesus doesn't respond with anger. Jesus doesn't get upset; but rather, Jesus simply makes an appeal to their faith and in His appeal, Jesus extends an invitation that would have them participate in the process

The Healing Experience

that would produce the healing experience that would change their lives. Jesus responds to their hurt with one request. Jesus asked them to simply show Him where they buried their brother. In other words, Jesus is interested and invested in being in the place where hurt is often insulated. This is where the Healing Experience begins. Whatever may be hurting you today, whatever hurt from your history that may be holding your life hostage in your current reality, whatever hurt is impacting and infecting you to the degree that it is manifesting symptoms in your attitude and behaviors towards others and even towards God, The Heavenly Father is making an appeal to your faith and is extending an invitation to you with the same request that He made to Mary and Martha.

If you are hurting and are ready for a healing experience, today the Heavenly Father says, "Show me where it hurts." Whatever hurt you are hiding and hoarding, whatever brokenness you have buried, whatever suffering you are suppressing, whatever disappointment you are disregarding, be encouraged in knowing that even today, the healing experience is available to you and all it takes is for you to honor God's request to trust Him enough to show Him where it hurts so He can help you experience the power of Healing that is not only available to you, but is your right and portion. This is where the process of our healing experience began in our marriage. After making the decision to fight for our marriage, we eventually got to a place with God where we could hear Him extend His invitation for us to show Him where we were hurting. You see, because of the finished and victorious work of Christ on the cross, we who are in relationship with Jesus Christ have healing as part of our inheritance, but that healing has to begin at the place of honoring God's request to show Him where it hurts.

The Healing Experience

A. Allow Access to the Address

Let's look further into the story of Mary and Martha's experience with hurt. We left off with Jesus making the request of them to show Him where they buried their brother. Let's pick it up from there: *34 "Where have you buried him?" he asked them. "Come and see, Lord," they answered. 38 Deeply moved once more, Jesus went to the tomb, which was a cave with a stone placed at the entrance. (John 11:34, 38)*

In this part of the experience, Jesus begins the process of the healing experience for Mary and Martha. You see, divine involvement will often wait for human invitation. Jesus has now been invited to the atmosphere of their agony. I want to suggest that healing requires God to be invited into the area or the address where our hurts began and may continue to exist. When they initially interacted with Jesus, the communication was compromised by the contamination of their hurt that was caused by the death of their brother. They were communicating, they were connecting to Jesus, but with all of the communication and conversation, Jesus was still confined to a distance from the actual area where the hurt existed. What this represents for us contextually is that sometimes, in order to experience authentic healing, we have to allow God to have access to the address of our agony. If you notice, both sisters communicated with Jesus, but in their communication, they never gave Jesus the opportunity to gain access to their agony. Let's paint that picture contextually. They communicate or they pray, but keep Jesus at bay so that they don't have to deal with the burden that they just buried. Sometimes, we can't get healed because even though we pray about it, we have not positioned God to personally participate in it. We keep things buried. We put up the self-protective walls. We lock the doors of our dysfunctional rooms and put up the "do not disturb" sign in order to deny anyone, including God,

The Healing Experience

the level of access that is needed to successfully deal with what is behind our closed doors. This is what the women were doing in their initial interaction with Jesus. The attitude of anger in their approach and in the way they addressed Jesus was simply a "do not disturb" sign that would result in Jesus being denied access to the address of their agony. If we took the time to honestly consider the attitudes that people often approach and address various situations in their lives and if we do the same honest assessment for our lives, we would likely have to conclude that we are often just like Mary and Martha. In our humanity, the natural tendency and proclivity is to protect our pain with privacy. On a larger scale of healing, consider again, the plight of the United States from the perspective of the social and racial unrest that is dominating the land. While many people communicate to God about the concern of the country's hurt, while many will pray that God heals the country and that the country will move forward in a more unified way so that it actually lives up to her name of being the United States of America, the truth is, for so long the country has not given God the level of access to the agony that would allow authentic healing to take place. We, in essence, have tried and continue to try living in a distorted and dysfunctional state of healing that simply buries the hurt to which God wants direct access. Again, this is simply the natural tendency to hide what will remind us and cause us to relive the hurt that we so desperately want to rid from our lives. The good news about God, is that God understands this proclivity for privatizing our pain. God understands our need to feel and be protected from having our pain publicized for others to witness. The conflict that is created in our need for protection that is presented in the privatization of our pain is that the pain eventually will pursue a platform so it can be presented in our daily performances. God understands that if the pain remains protected by our privacy, that protection builds a prison

The Healing Experience

for prevailing progress. Because God's love prioritizes liberation, God will not idly sit back and allow us to privatize our pain, particularly when our pain is presenting itself in our daily performances. This is why Jesus made the request for the sisters to show Him where they buried their hurt. They had to give Him access in order for them to experience the healing that was available to them. So when they responded to The Lord's request to show Him where it hurts by taking Jesus to the tomb, they in essence were making the decision to let God deal with the hurt that was hidden. There are some hurting experiences that we can't just pray about, but we must make a decision to give God the kind of access to where the hurt lives because that becomes the invitation that influences a more intimate involvement from God. While it's understandable that we have difficulty allowing people to have access to where we hurt, if healing is going to happen, we have to at least develop the kind of relationship with God where we trust God with the level of clearance needed to deal with our hurts. Oftentimes with people, we present what we perceive others deem as presentable and if we're not careful, we will put those same parameters up that will even deny God permission to help us heal. Now, let's talk a little more about what caused them to allow Jesus to have access to the address of their agony. There are 2 main reasons why Jesus was given access to their hurt. The first is **Connection**.

Connection speaks of their relationship with Jesus. Remember, this family was deeply connected to Jesus and so they were comfortable giving Jesus the access that he needed to help deal with their hurts. If you think about it, no rational person is going to give a stranger complete access to their hidden places. Even if there is a connection, if that connection is weak, you will be limited in your access to that person's private places. Even a cell phone will give you limited access if there is a weak connection. If our connection to God

The Healing Experience

is lacking or underdeveloped, we will have a hard time giving God the access that is needed to address the hurts where they live. This is why developing our relationship with God is so important. Like any relationship, trust is developed in times of togetherness. You start to develop more trust in people when you are able to spend more time with them. The more we engage in a growing relationship with God, the more comfortable we will become with giving God access to our hurting address. Consider going to the doctor's office for a checkup. Some people will go to their doctor knowing something is wrong, but they would rather keep the pain or the concern hidden rather than give the doctor access to the area that is causing their pain. The same principle exists in counseling. Some people will go to counseling, but they struggle to provide information that would help the counselor be more effective in helping them with their concerns.

When Chaka and I decided to fight for our marriage, our connection to God was the only source that made it possible for us to even fight that kind of fight. It was our relationship with God individually that gave us the comfort level to even begin talking about the details of our marriage. In these various encounters, we would often pray and do our best to begin showing God where we thought the hurts were. This was extremely helpful because our communication with God allowed us to talk about it. With God, we could at least begin the process of opening the door with our words that would create the possibility of an exit place for our hurts.

You see, regardless of the hurt, healing requires access to the area or the address of where the hurt exists. The healing experience is going to require the kind of access that will tell God "this is where it hurts." Sometimes, we just have to tell God, "My heart hurts" or "my mind hurts" or "what happened in my childhood still hurts." The second reason the sisters are able to give Jesus access to their hurting address

The Healing Experience

is because of their **Convictions.** They were convinced that not only did Jesus care about them, but Jesus developed a conviction in them of His capacity to help them heal. You see, prior to taking Jesus to the tomb, Jesus dealt directly with their convictions or their faith in Him. Let's go back and review the initial interaction found in verses 20-27:

> *"When Martha heard that Jesus was coming, she went out to meet him, but Mary stayed in the house. Martha said to Jesus, "If you had been here, Lord, my brother would not have died! But I know that even now God will give you whatever you ask him for." "Your brother will rise to life," Jesus told her. "I know," she replied, "that he will rise to life on the last day." Jesus said to her, "I am the resurrection and the life. Those who believe in me will live, even though they die; and those who live and believe in me will never die. Do you believe this?" "Yes, Lord!" she answered. "I do believe that you are the Messiah, the Son of God, who was to come into the world.""* John 11:20-27 GNT

In this part of the experience, we can clearly see that Martha has strong convictions about Jesus. She is convinced, she has faith that Jesus has authority to make reservations for the dead to go to heaven. She also reveals that part of her convictions about Jesus is that Jesus is able to bring the relief of healing to those who are sick on earth. While those are strong convictions, they have constraints that would compromise the conclusion that Jesus had the capacity to create, which would result in the healing experience they needed for their lives. Notice their convictions. For them, if someone is sick, Jesus can

The Healing Experience

help them get well. If someone dies, Jesus can help them get into heaven. However, if someone dies, they have no convictions that address whether or not Jesus can transition someone from a state of death back to a state of life on earth. As a result of this constraint or this limitation in their convictions or their faith, Jesus takes the time to confront the constraint in order to create the conclusion that was needed for healing to be completed. Jesus responds to their conviction constraint by presenting them a deeper revelation of who He is. He gives them a level of insight that would then increase their faith to the level needed for them to trust Jesus with the address of their agony. After Jesus provides the revelation that He is the resurrection, that He also has authority over death, He challenges Martha to believe the revelation. Martha responded to Jesus by raising her faith. Because of this new level of conviction, Jesus was given the necessary level of clearance that was conducive to the intended conclusion. You see, convictions can create the conditions of clearance we give to God and people.

So, when Jesus makes the request that they show Him where they buried the body of their brother, Martha was able to give Jesus access to the address. She takes him to the place where their hurt was being held. This is critical to the healing experience. Jesus has to be present in the places where we are experiencing our pain. Now, how do we do that today? What Martha demonstrates is that your faith that exists must become a faith that is expressed. We know her faith increased because she expressed words that agreed with the revelation that Jesus provided. She said, *I believe*. Regardless of the hurts we may have and regardless of the area that is experiencing hurt, if we are going to give Jesus access to the hurt, we must transition our faith from a state of existence to a state of expression. You have to express faith at the place where the hurt exists. If you're experiencing hurt in your

The Healing Experience

marriage or hurt from your childhood, begin to express your convictions or your faith in a way that confronts the hurt you are experiencing. Whether your expression is in the form of the words you speak or the worship you offer or even the works that you demonstrate, just direct the expression of your faith towards the place where your hurts exist. This will create an atmosphere that gives God's presence access to the places where we hurt in life. If we really want to experience healing that heaven can provide, then we have to make sure that heaven has access to our hurts. Sometimes, that means, when we are experiencing hurts, we may need to begin worshipping God with that particular hurt in mind. It may mean that we may have to intentionally begin thinking about what is hurting and allow that hurt to come to the surface. While it is at the surface of our thoughts and our emotions, we fill the atmosphere with praise and worship music. It may mean combating the thoughts and the pain with intense and intentional prayer and meditative focus on the love of God. Whatever you must do in order to express your faith in a way that helps create an atmosphere that is welcoming to the presence of God, then that is what you must do in order to give God access to the address of your hurt. What we will discover is that, just being in God's presence when we are hurting will do wonders for our healing experience. It was this conviction of who God is for us and what God was able to do in our marriage that allowed us to continue fighting even when it seemed like we just weren't going to make it. Because of our convictions, we would consistently show God our hurts through the vehicle of spoken or written prayers to God, worshipping God, reading and meditating on God's Word. Every chance we had, we would usher God's presence into the places of our pain. This process of giving God's presence access empowered us to continue trying to work towards healing together. When we give God's presence access to where we hurt, we will discover that God's presence alone can spark something inside of us. God's presence alone can begin the process of freeing us from the grip and grasp of our hurts. There is a level of freedom that only God's presence can provide. The bible reminds of this when it tells us that where the Spirit of the Lord is, there is liberty. When you take His presence to your hurts, God will begin the process of exchanging your mourning into dancing and your sorrows into joy. If we are serious about showing God where it hurts so we can have a real healing experience, we have to develop the level of connection with and convictions about God that makes us comfortable enough to allow God to have access to the address of our hurts so we can experience the healing that we need.

B. Correction at the Core

Once we make the decision to trust God with access to our hurts, we must then trust God to make the necessary corrections at the core of our hurts. As a matter of fact, the reason God wants us to give Him access is because God wants to correct the cause that's at the core of our hurts. Let's go further into the experience that Mary and Martha are having with Jesus.

> *39 "Take the stone away!" Jesus ordered. Martha, the dead man's sister, answered, "There will be a bad smell, Lord. He has been buried four days!" 40 Jesus said to her, "Didn't I tell you that you would see God's glory if you believed?" 41 They took the*

The Healing Experience

> *stone away. Jesus looked up and said, "I thank you, Father, that you listen to me. 42 I know that you always listen to me, but I say this for the sake of the people here, so that they will believe that you sent me." 43 After he had said this, he called out in a loud voice, "Lazarus, come out!" John 11:39-43 GNT*

Just a few verses ago, there was a willingness to take Jesus to the tomb. Jesus was given access to the address of their pain. But now, there's a problem, because Jesus is not satisfied with access. Jesus wants to address the agony. Jesus wants to deal with the hurt so He can use His healing power to correct the core issue. When they get to the tomb, Jesus instructs them to take the stone away because the stone was keeping Jesus from being able to deal with the dead body, which was at the core of their hurt. You see, the tomb represents the address of the hurt, but the body represents the actuality of the hurt; it represents the core. The tomb represents the generality of our hurts, but the body represents the specificity of our hurts. Jesus wanted access to the body, so he could deal with the specific hurt. He wanted to get to the root of the pain.

Sometimes, we approach God with generalities, when God is looking for specificities. God wants specifics, not generalities, because the generalities reveal that there is still a part of us that struggles to trust God with our transparency. Yet transparency is absolutely critical to experiencing corrections at the core. As long as the core is not being corrected, the experience of healing can't be completed because there will be constraints crafted by the contamination of our hurts.

If we are serious about having our healing experiences, we must become open to correction being done at the core of the matter. The

The Healing Experience

only reason that God wants us to even show Him where we are hurting is so that He can correct the cause of the hurt so that healing becomes the conclusion. God is not trying to be nosey in requesting our transparency. God wants to correct the core and in order to correct the core, God will have to confront and combat the very cause of the hurt. This is what Jesus demonstrates when he gives the directive to take the stone away because the stone symbolizes challenges that keep the core from being confronted, which then keeps it from being corrected. When healing is the goal, we have to be willing to trust God enough to not only connect Him to the core, but trust Him to correct the core. It's one thing to give God access to it, but with that access, are you willing to submit to God's authority to help correct what is hurting you.

    I was sitting in my office one day and a couple, who weren't members of the church that I Pastored, walked in. Their presence and their posture immediately revealed that they needed help with their marriage. After praying, I opened up the conversation by asking them how I could be of assistance. The wife began telling me about the trouble they were having as a married couple and they just needed help. The husband barely said anything. I began to ask questions about their marriage and while the wife was willing to speak her hurt, the husband shielded himself by shutting down. I began to notice as one spoke freely and the other one spoke cautiously, both were able to show me where they were hurting. The wife expressed how the husband was hurting her and the husband expressed what the wife was doing to hurt him. They both were hurting and based on what they expressed verbally, they both were willing to take me to the tombs of their marriage, but they struggled to take me inside of the tomb and connect me to the core of their condition. I eventually told the couple that while I would love to help and while I believe God can mend any broken matter in their lives, until they both became ready enough to be

The Healing Experience

transparent and honest in answering some questions, until they were comfortable enough to connect me to their core, then I would be constrained from providing the kind of correction that would cultivate healing in their marriage. In essence, what I was asking them to do collectively was take the stones away. Both of them were using their perspective of the marital condition to conceal the real causes that existed at the core of their condition.

If authentic healing is what we desire, we have to be willing to break down the barriers that are blocking us from dealing with our brokenness. One of the greatest challenges to experiencing healing in my marriage was our struggle to remove the stones so that we could begin to discover what stood beneath the surface of our struggles. You see, this represents an intentional decision to move beyond the pain at the surface and dive deep to discover what exists beneath the behavior that has caused so much pain. In the beginning of our attempts to restore our marriage, we had to deal with the shock, the feelings of betrayal, the excuse making, the rage, and eventually the constant back-and-forth arguing that occurred. All of these were responses that represented symptoms of the significant level of hurt that existed beneath the behaviors we were displaying towards one another. What these behavioral responses also indicated was that neither one of us were ready to fully remove the stones and as a result, our marriage functioned in a rollercoaster state for years.

In the United States, for centuries, the evil history of slavery and the continued reality of racism has been part of the brokenness that has been buried and blocked from being dealt with in a way that makes healing possible. The healing that is needed in this country and in those who are experiencing hurt individually requires that we be willing to disengage the defense mechanisms that we use to protect ourselves from having to deal with the core of the matter. We can't continue to

The Healing Experience

have communication and conversation that circumvents the causes at the core of our contextual conditions. We must have transparent and vulnerable conversations and even more, conversations that will help charter a course towards correction. If healing is the goal, then we can no longer accept the causes at the core to reside in concealment and confinement; they must be confronted and corrected in order to conclude in authentic healing. In essence, the directive to those who want to experience healing is to begin the process of rolling the stones away. As long as the stones are allowed to stay, suffering will continue to be suppressed, which eventually will sabotage any level of success that one tries to establish.

Now, the removal of stones presents a difficult process and thus helps give understanding to why it is often difficult to experience healing for various experiences of pain. I've discovered that one pivotal factor that perpetuates pain is a distorted perception of self-protection. We are simply trying to protect ourselves. We keep the stones in their place because it provides a sense of security from our suffering. It allows the suffering to shift into a state of suppression, thus removing it from the surface, so that it is no longer in plain sight. The stone enables us to move forward believing that since the hurt is no longer in our faces, we are free to move into our future. As a result, we are able to function and even try to flourish in our lives, because the stone has provided us this security. The problem with that approach to healing is that while the visibility of the hurtful experience is removed, the venom that the experience creates will remain; and eventually, what remains, will be revealed and bring ruining results into your reality. If healing is the prize we are after, then the stones must be removed. Healing requires transparency, which will leave us in a state of vulnerability. Regardless of the security the stones may seem to symbolize in your life, if you want real healing, you have to be willing to take the stone away.

Now, notice in their interaction with Jesus, Jesus tells THEM to take the stone away. Jesus could have easily removed the stone Himself. Jesus could have easily spoken to the stone and it would have had to move out of the way. Jesus doesn't do that. Rather, he calls them to do it, because the healing experience requires that the one who needs healing participates in the process of receiving healing. This part of the process God won't do for us, but He will wait until we do it for ourselves. If God removes it, then God is forcing it upon us; but if healing is what we really want, then we've got to get the stone removed. Jesus will provide the revelation that it needs to be removed, but the removal is our responsibility. We have to give authorization and approval to remove what is blocking access to the core of our hurting experiences. This removing process is where things get very challenging for Mary and Martha and it gets challenging for us today. In the biblical experience with Mary and Martha, Martha reveals in vs. 39 why the removal process is so difficult. The verse says, *Martha, the dead man's sister, answered, "There will be a bad smell, Lord. He has been buried four days!"* For Martha, the stone was protecting her and Mary from having to deal with the contamination beyond the stone.

Sometimes, the hurts we can experience in life can get so deep and they can be in place for so long that contamination is cultivated. With that contamination also comes signs and symptoms that indicate there is something that is contaminated. Behind the stone, was a contaminated body, but with that contaminated body, there was also a contaminated smell that would immediately give attention to that contaminated body. Do you see why the stone was so important for them? As long as the stone was there, no one would be able to experience the horrendous stench of death, which then would also keep

The Healing Experience

concealed the real problem lying at the core of their condition. You see, the deeper we dig behind or beneath the stones of our lives, the less distance there is from the dysfunction of our lives that is being hidden by the stones we put in place. I know families and marriages and friendships today who look healthy on the surface, but are hurting in secret and they are comfortable with that. They are comfortable in their current conditions. They have learned how to co-exist with the conditions they are experiencing. They would rather things stay as they are instead of trying to work towards the kind of healing that may request and require them to remove the stones. There are generations of people who have approached hurt with the "sweep it under the rug" mentality. They have insulated the experiences that have hurt them for so long that now they are afraid that people and even they themselves, won't be able to handle the infection that may exist and may have evolved from all of the years they have insulated their hurt. They are afraid of the odor that may be exposed, which would also expose the contamination at the core.

 The truth of the matter is, sometimes, when you are in the process of trying to experience healing, people will get offended by your odor. People may not be able to handle the stinky seasons of your healing process. The more we choose to remove the stones, the more people may choose to remove themselves from our lives and we have to accept that reality. The healing experience will test and try the strength of our relationships. If the relationship or the connection isn't strong enough, it may not survive your process towards receiving a healing experience. During the healing experience, it becomes critical that we are careful about the company we keep around us because some people may disconnect from us when the dysfunction becomes too much for them to deal with. This can create a challenge because if we're not careful, we can end up compromising our healing in order to continue

The Healing Experience

connections and companionships with people who can't handle our contamination. When healing is the goal, it is important to have the right people in your corner. Healing is not only challenging for the one who needs healing, but it is also challenging for those who are called to be healing support systems. The wrong support will stifle your success.

In Mary and Martha's experience, they were obviously blessed to have Jesus in their corner. Jesus was not offended by the odor of their hurt. Jesus was not concerned about the smell of the body. He understood that the smell was just a surface symptom that served as a sign pointing to the real source of their suffering. The source of the suffering was not the odor and it was not their attitude, but rather it was their brother, who experienced death in his body that served as the source of their suffering. Their brother being dead was the core that needed to be corrected. This correction is critical to the healing experience. Healing must address the core of the matter. Jesus goes after the core, but notice before He deals with the core, He gives her support by reminding her of the faith she had just expressed that agreed with His capacity to deal with her hurt. I love Jesus, because he always demonstrates the love and compassion that He has for us. He never condemns her or gets frustrated by her lack of faith. Rather, He stabilizes her faith. You see, during the process towards healing, it is critical that our faith not only elevates but that it endures until we experience the healing that God desires us to experience.

The deeper we go into the process and the longer we go through the process, the more critical it will be for our faith to be present in the process. When you are going through the process of healing, find ways to stabilize your faith in God. Find ways to feed your faith so that the facts don't overwhelm you into doubt and disbelief. After restabilizing her faith, Jesus moves forward with the opportunity to operate at the root of their pain. With the stone now removed, Jesus was free to bring

The Healing Experience

correction to the core. At the core of their hurting condition, was the death of their brother. To correct the core, Jesus calls out to Lazarus and tells him to come out. The application for us is this: In order to correct the core, we must cultivate the change we want to see with corresponding conduct. Jesus wanted to cultivate a change from death to life, so He confronts the core with conduct that will correspond to the change that He wants to create. He speaks words of life, which then collides with the condition of death and as a result, resurrection and revitalization takes place. How does that look for us today? If you are hurting and you have identified the core of the matter, if you have an awareness of the core condition that is causing the hurt that you are experiencing, then that core has to be corrected and the correcting of the core requires us to engage in conduct or actions that correspond or concur or agree with the change we want to cultivate in our lives. Again, this is difficult and draining work. It is even more difficult if you aren't even aware of the issues that exist at the core. For Mary and Martha, they were aware that their brother had died. They knew what was behind the stone. For many of us, there are times when we find ourselves living and functioning with stones in place and we have no idea why. We don't know why our attitudes are the way they are. We don't know why we behave the way we do. We have no clue as to why we respond to people the way we do. We aren't aware of what exists behind the stones of our behaviors. And because we are not even aware of what exists behind the stones, not to mention, aware that the stones are even in place, we don't have the capacity to roll the stones away. As a result, the core never gets confronted because we don't have the necessary connections that will help us remove the stones.

When Chaka and I began our journey towards our healing experience, we had no idea that we would discover all of these causes as the core of our hurts. We were living and trying to love each other

The Healing Experience

with stones in place. We weren't even aware that stones were in place. We just assumed these behaviors and responses were just a part of who we were and now they are coming to the forefront of the relationship. While we did what we could to support ourselves spiritually, it wasn't until we sought out certain connections that our stones began to be rolled away. God led us to connections such as our spiritual covering, mentors, professional counselors and healing ministries. One organization that I want to recommend highly is called Restoring The Foundations. They help provide an integrated approach to the ministry of healing and freedom. After establishing and thoroughly engaging these connections, the stones were rolling away and that gave God the level of access needed to bring correction to the core of the hurts we were experiencing in our marriage. Through the various support systems that helped roll the stones away, we discovered that all of the arguing, all of the moments of wanting to quit and throw in the towel, all of the venom and vitriol that we allowed to be spewed into our marriage were the various stones and odors that eventually exposed a variety of core issues that made its way into our marriage. Issues such as childhood molestation, abandonment, rejection, fatherlessness, no self-worth, self-sabotage, and much more all were discovered at the core of our hurts.

The conduct or the actions that we engage in to cultivate change will be different based on the contamination that is at the core. If I'm dealing with abuse as the core of what is causing my hurt, then to correct the core, I have to do something about the abuse that's going to result in the safety and love that I want to see as the counter to the abuse I've been experiencing. That may require me to leave the relationship and even place a restraining order if necessary. If rejection is the core that needs to be corrected, then I have to engage in conduct or behavior or actions that will cultivate a change from feeling rejected

The Healing Experience

to feeling received and accepted for who I am. That may require a change in my social circle. That may require me engulfing myself in God's thoughts concerning me. If racial inequality is the cause at the core, then I need to engage in processes that will result in the implementation of behaviors and policies that encourage and enforce real equality, inclusion and love. That may require me to engage in cultural sensitivity training, candid and compassionate conversations, Holy Spirit-influenced biblical application, and civic responsibilities, such as voting for candidates who prioritize correcting racial inequality.

Again, that corresponding conduct will look different based on the situation. For some, that conduct may simply be consistent self-affirmation or connecting with people who love and value me enough to provide positive affirmation of who I am. To correct the core, you may need the corresponding conduct of disconnecting from negative people. Correcting the core may require professional counseling. Regardless of the conduct or actions or methods we use to cultivate the change that corrects the core, what is most important is that we confront the core and correct it so that we are no longer controlled by it. If you are reading this book and you are aware of the core that is causing hurt in your life, I want to challenge you to begin praying and seeking God about ways you can cultivate the change you want to see. Begin to list actions you can take that can help bring correction to the core that is causing your hurt. Do you need to disconnect from some people? Do you need a change of scenery? Could professional counseling assist in bringing healing into your life? Would engaging in a deeper prayer life cultivate the change you need? Take time to honestly assess the hurts that you are experiencing and begin to seek out ways that you can attack the core of the matter with actions that can achieve the correction that will lead to your healing experience.

C. Stripping Away Symbols of Suffering

Once we have given God access to the address of our hearts that allows God to correct the core of the matter, healing will begin to take place. Now with the healing that is happening, it is going to be critical for us to help maximize the healing process by stripping away any symbols of our suffering. Again, let's continue to engage the experience that these sisters are having in our scripture reference. So far, we have gotten to the place in their experience, where Jesus corrects the core by commanding life back into Lazarus. Jesus uses the authority of His Words to cultivate the conclusion of life that He wanted to see. Let's pick it back up at verse 43 and continue into verse 44:

> *43 After he had said this, he called out in a loud voice, "Lazarus, come out!" 44 He came out, his hands and feet wrapped in grave cloths, and with a cloth around his face. "Untie him," Jesus told them, "and let him go." John 11:43-44 GNT*

Again, healing is happening, not only for Lazarus, but for Mary and Martha as well. Jesus has corrected the core. At His command, at the authority of His word, a miracle was manifested and Lazarus was brought back to life and came out of the tomb. The source of the hurt was healed. Now, it is important to understand that while healing is needed, while we may pray and believe God for a healing experience, God ultimately decides what the healing experience will look like in our lives. For the family in our text, the picture and production of

The Healing Experience

healing consisted of Lazarus being resurrected from a state of death. For some of us, the healing experience may not always consist of the conclusions that we may be seeking from God. For example, The Apostle Paul prayed three times for God to remove what he referred to as "a thorn in his side." While he never specifies what that thorn was, his prayer for God to remove implies that He was seeking some healing experience or some form of correction to whatever the condition may have been. Paul lets us know that God never removed it; God never healed it; at least not in accordance to the picture or production of healing that Paul was seeking. While God never removed it, Paul lets us know that He is better with that weakness because in that weakness, He is stronger; because that weakness ensures a level of reliability on God that allows the power of God to be made evident through the weakness of Paul's thorn, that God did not deal with according to Paul's desire. There are many people who pray for various forms of a healing experiences and we have in our mind what we want the outcome to look like. We pray for healing in our marriage and we expect the marriage to recover and last only to have the experience of divorce interrupt the journey. While they prayed for a healing experience, the divorce may not be the sign that God didn't provide a healing experience, but maybe, just maybe, the divorce was the form of disconnection necessary in order for one or both individuals to have the healing experience that their lives needed. Again, for Mary, Martha and Lazarus, Jesus determined that their healing experience would consist of Lazarus being resurrected back to life. At this point, they are having their healing experience. The problem, however, is that Lazarus, while being resurrected from the dead, his face, hands and feet were still bound with grave clothes. This illustrates the residual impact of the hurt that was experienced in the form of his death. Jesus provides a healing experience that is not yet complete because while Lazarus is

The Healing Experience

alive, he is still living bound. Here is the impact his bondage would have on the sisters. If Lazarus remained bound, Mary and Martha would be stuck in a relationship with someone who has lost vision as symbolized by the face being covered; they would be stuck in a relationship with someone who has lost their ability to be productive as symbolized by the hands being bound; and they would be stuck in a relationship with someone who has lost their mobility or their ability to make progress in life. In other words, they are tied to someone who has no direction, no production and no progression in life. How effective would the healing experience be if Jesus only raised him back to life, but left him in a condition where the quality of his life would be diminished? How effective is the healing if God heals your marriage to the point that you don't want a divorce, but you struggle to be with the person to whom you are married? This is what the family would have had to face if the healing experience only brought Lazarus back to life. What this shows us is, sometimes, while it is important to correct the core of matter, we can't ignore how the hurt could have impacted every area of our lives. Lazarus is bound face, hands and feet with grave clothes. The clothes are significant because they represent symbols of our suffering. They represent triggers of our turmoil. You see, the healing experience has resulted in his recovery, but it can't stop at his recovery, but it must now deal with the reminders of his ruined reality. When we are going through our healing experiences, we have to understand we can't just stop at the point of recovery, but we must also do the work of removing the reminders of our ruined reality. If healing is going to be effective, it must consist of the stripping away and the separation of symbols that may work to keep us in a suffering state. In this biblical family's healing experience, what we see is that God is able to heal just at the authority of His word. Healing is never the problem for God; however if the symbols of our suffering aren't

The Healing Experience

removed, then the suffering will remain even though the source of the suffering is no longer our reality. Mary and Martha would have continued to suffer in their relationship with Lazarus, not because Lazarus was still in a state of death, but because Lazarus still had symbols of his death that had not yet been stripped away or separated from his life. Now, remember, his face, his hands and his feet are bound with grave clothes. His vision or direction in life, his capacity for production and progression is bound by grave clothes. What that means is, for Lazarus, every time he would try to establish vision or direction for his life, it would be influenced by the death he experienced, because all he would be able to see are the grave clothes covering his face. Similarly, every time Lazarus would try to produce something or try to make progress in his life, he would be impacted and influenced by the death he experienced, which would limit his production and progression to dead results. As a pastor, I've had many spiritual counseling sessions with people who struggled with moving forward in their lives, because they could not get past the experiences that they were no longer dealing with, but were still being dominated by. This is the challenge that is presented at the tomb. Healing has taken place, but healing is incomplete if bondage is not broken. For those of us who are serious about healing, we have to understand that any authentic healing experience must also include the work of liberation or freedom or deliverance. Jesus engages in the ministry of deliverance or liberation in order to complete the healing experience for this family. This speaks to the fact that God is not only interested in our healing, but He is interested in us being made whole. The healing experience is about wholeness. Lazarus was healed but there would be no wholeness without the liberating work of deliverance. This principle is critical for those of us who are in need of the healing experience. We have to be willing to go beyond just doing the work of healing and begin to do the

The Healing Experience

work that will also result in deliverance or freedom. Now, let's look at the story again and see how the work of liberation and deliverance was done in order to maximize the healing experience. In vs. 44 of this story, it says, *44 He came out, his hands and feet wrapped in grave cloths, and with a cloth around his face. "Untie him," Jesus told them, "and let him go."* Notice the work of liberating Lazarus from the grave clothes. Jesus tells "them" to untie him and let him go. Notice that similar to the work of removing the stone, God puts this work of liberation on the shoulders of human participation. The element of human participation is absolutely essential to the experience of emancipation. This is an example of what I call "Collaborative Theology." I define Collaborative theology, as the divine processing and response towards the plight of humanity by way of divine partnership with humanity. You see, there are levels of freedom and liberation that can't be experienced without the collaboration of divinity and humanity. While God could easily do all of the work for us, God chooses to partner with us in the process of our own progress. I remember right after hurricane Katrina devastated New Orleans, a group of seminarians from The School of Theology at Virginia Union University felt compelled to travel to New Orleans and help provide a measure of healing and restoration to that community. While in New Orleans, we saw firsthand, the devastation and destruction that the hurricane caused. We partnered with some local pastors and local construction workers to provide physical restoration in the form of a demolition team and then spiritual restoration in the form of ministry counseling to victims of that storm. One night during our debrief, everyone was going around the table discussing the impact of what they experienced throughout that day. Many, if not all of us, were discouraged by what we experienced. At that debrief session, many expressed not only their discouragement, but also their feelings of

The Healing Experience

disappointment in a God whom we have determined to be absent in the recovery process. Collectively, we all wrestled with the question, where is God in the rebuilding process. Collectively, we all wondered if the feeling of abandonment that Jesus expressed on the cross was applicable to our attempts to help provide a measure of healing to the victims that we encountered. All of a sudden, while we were giving God and one another our transparency, God began to speak to me and I, along with others began to share that while God may not have provided any kind of mystical or supernatural assistance that we were knowledgeable about, the truth of the matter is, throughout the rebuilding process, throughout our recovery effort, God has maintained His consistency of being a very present help in the time of trouble. I told the group that while we can't see God's hands working, what we do have is a representation of God's hands working through our hands. We have become the demonstration of God's heart and God's hands at work in helping to bring about recovery. While God didn't provide any supernatural assistance, God did speak to our hearts and the hearts of many who are supporting our work and that partnership is providing a level of production that only God can only result in God getting the glory. You see, whenever there is a need for the fullness of healing, human participation is always required. Jesus is going to ask us to remove stones and to remove the grave clothes that are keeping people bound. There are some symbols that will only be stripped away or we will only be able to separate from if we do the work ourselves or if we have the right support system to help set us free. If we really want God to provide a healing experience in our lives, we have to do the work of getting freed or getting delivered from things that trigger or remind us of our hurt. It is important to emphasize that this work of stripping away the symbols, this work of getting freed or delivered from the triggers and reminders of our hurt will often require support systems. It

The Healing Experience

will often require help beyond your own hands. As a matter of fact, most of the time, the symbols can be so suppressing that it will stifle us from tapping into the strength we need to set ourselves free. That's why Jesus doesn't tell Lazarus to remove his own grave clothes, but he tells "them" because he is in a position where he doesn't have the power to free himself. He needs help. The level of healing that God wants us to experience requires us to get help from others in order to do the work that will maximize the healing experience that is needed. You may be asking, "Well, what does that work entail?" The first part of the work of freedom or deliverance is **Recognition**. If we are going to get freedom or deliverance from symbols of our suffering, we must at least be able to recognize the symbols. We must be able to identify what those triggers are. Take some time to begin identifying what is it that when you see it and when you get around it, it becomes a reminder for you of the hurt you went through; what is it that makes you relive the hurt and won't let the hurt leave your life? What is it that keeps your hands and feet tied to doing stuff and going to places that resemble and look like the places that hurt you? What is it that keeps your face covered in the shame and guilt of what you went through; what is it that keeps your mind covered in the hurt to the degree that you can't even function properly, to the degree that you sabotage any opportunity of success for your life because your mind is still impacted by the hurt you experienced? And for many of us, it's not what, but it's who! Who is it in your life that seems to have you tied hand and feet in the hurt you experienced because of them? Who is it that no matter what you do, you just can't get free from them or no matter how hard you try, your mind is consumed and covered by thoughts of them? Again, this part of the work will often require the help of others. Sometimes, you need people who can help you identify or point out behaviors that can probably be traced back to a thought or a trigger of some kind. Once

The Healing Experience

the symbol is recognized, the next part of the work requires the **Removal** process. Jesus instructs them to untie Lazarus. Remove it off of him. In other words, Jesus is telling them to help Lazarus deal with the symbols until they no longer can detain him. Help him rid his life of those symbols until they can no longer suppress his success in life. Help remove the symbols that are covering his face or his vision and direction in life with past trauma and tragedy. Remove the symbols that are preventing him from being productive according to his potential in life. Remove the symbols that are preventing him from making the kind of progress that would satisfy his purpose in life. Again, this requires support. This requires help beyond our own hands. This level of deliverance or freedom requires us to connect to support systems that can help us do the work of removing the symbols out of your lives. Another critical part of the work of deliverance or freedom is the process of **Release**. This part of the work is represented by the instructions to "let him go." Sometimes, deliverance requires a release. The release is unique because this part of the deliverance or freedom process is not about the symbols, but it's about the support systems in our lives. Jesus tells "them" to let him go. The inference here is that the people whom he keeps in his space will also have a say in the experience of his deliverance. Sometimes, the reason we struggle to be free and stay free is not simply because of symbols, but rather it's because we may have the wrong support. What this speaks to is, we have to be careful of having support or being support to others that will hinder release with reminders. Sometimes, there are people in our lives who love us and mean us well, but they always seem to try to hold us hostage to our hurts by constantly bringing up our hurts. Sometimes, the support system can stifle deliverance. If you have people around you who carry unforgiveness because of what you went through, if you're not careful, their unforgiveness can become a symbol of the

The Healing Experience

suffering that you have been trying to get removed out of your life. This happens quite a bit in relationships. Here you are trying to move forward from hurtful experiences. The problem is, the friend you shared it with refuses to let you forget it even though you are ready to move forward from it. The work of deliverance is going to require that friend and those whom we keep in our spaces, to release us or to let us go so that we aren't constantly having to relive the hurt through the symbol of their unforgiveness.

At the end of the day, if we desire the healing experience that God has made available and accessible to us, that experience requires collaboration between God and man. God will do what only God can do, but there must be a level of human participation if the healing experience is going to produce the best results possible. We can't just show God where it hurts and allow God to correct the core while we sit back and do nothing. We must become active participants in our healing experience. We must be open enough to allow others to become support systems that can help us seize and sustain healing success. And let me also emphasize, that when it comes to the support systems that we rely on to help us strip away the symbols of suffering so we can sustain our healing, it is important to make sure that the support system is well rounded in their experience and expertise. If you are hurting today or if you are trying to experience healing from your hurts, while God is the source of your support, while God is the foundation, begin to pray about other bricks that you can lay to help build a strong support system in your life. Don't singularize the kind of support you keep in your space. Again, when Chaka and I were going through our healing experience, it was this understanding of support systems that really shifted us towards healing results we continue to enjoy and thrive in today. Ask God to show you who you can tap into spiritually, professionally, socially. Your healing may require spiritual

The Healing Experience

support from your Pastor or church community; but it may also require the support of professional counseling or a life coach. Your healing may require support from your Spouse or loving family members or friends. I trust and believe that if you seek God for the right support system to help you with your healing experience, God will send suitable support into your life who will help you strip away the symbols of your suffering so you can both seize and sustain your healing experience.

Child of God, if you've gotten this far into the book, my prayer is that you have already gained understanding of God's heart for you to have the healing experience that you need. It is my prayer that you have become or are becoming open enough with God to show God where you hurt. If you have gotten this far, I decree and declare over your life that God is providing you with the grace to be bold enough to roll the stones away; I decree that in this season of your life, God is giving you the strength and sending support into your life to help you roll stones away and knock down walls and dismantle defense mechanisms that have been developed to disguise and deny the existence of hurt that has been damaging and dominating your life.

As you read this book, I come against the fear that creates costumes and cover ups that conceal even from God what His power is able to correct for our greater good. I decree that if you remain committed to showing God where it hurts, God's hand will begin to handle the heart of the matter to ensure the maximum performance and production of The Healing Experience in your life.

The Healing Experience

The Healing Experience Notes:

_____

_____

_____

_____

_____

_____

_____

_____

_____

_____

_____

_____

_____

_____

_____

CHAPTER TWO

FINDING VICTORY IN VULNERALBILITY

Earlier in this book, I mentioned a pastoral care experience with Jacob and Rachel at their kitchen table. This experience was only the beginning. Eventually, they both would share the hurt they were experiencing in their marriage. What was quite striking to me was how well composed both seemed to be when sharing their hurt. The experiences seemed extreme, but their emotions lacked the level of expression that one would expect to demonstrate going through the experiences that both of them have gone through and were going through at that time. With Rachel, the emotional expression was clearly demonstrated by her discouraged and depressing disposition. Jacob, on the other hand, was initially calm, cool and collective when sharing the hurt he was trying to handle at that moment. As we continued to have these pastoral care experiences, I began to notice a shift in Jacob's emotional expression. As he continued to share his personal experiences about where he was in his life and the traumatic experiences he has endured through since childhood, Jacob's emotions were no longer being enclosed, but they were being expressed. Jacob and Rachel had both reached a level of vulnerability that would help them find victory over their hurts. One of the greatest support

The Healing Experience

mechanisms for the healing experience is our willingness to stand in the power of our vulnerability. You see, while showing God where we hurt is critical to the healing experience, I want to suggest that equally as important as showing God "where" we hurt is our willingness to show God "that" we hurt. You see, one of the reasons Jacob and Rachel struggled to experience healing early on was because while they were willing to acknowledge what was hurting and where the hurt was, they never allowed themselves to experience the healing power of expressing their hurt the right way. Their previous expressions were dictated and dominated by the infections that resulted from hurts that they have insulated for so long. Their expressions were under the control of their hurts that had contaminated their conduct. If healing is going to be experienced, we have to be willing to engage the level of vulnerability that will empower us to express our emotions in a way that is conducive to the healing experience that will bring us into a state of victory in our lives. While it may not be comfortable, our vulnerability is critical to experiencing the kind of healing that can help lead to a victorious life. Again, one of the greatest elements and examples that give evidence to the authenticity of our vulnerability is a healthy engagement of emotional expressivity. If we can tap into a level of vulnerability that allows us to express our emotions in a healthy way, especially to God, then we position ourselves in a great way to experience a level of victory over our hurts that, only the healing experience could provide. One example of an effective element of emotional expression is the release of our tears. Have you ever considered why God created us with the capacity to cry? In her article written for The American Academy of Ophthalmology, Dr. Reena Mukamal says this about our tears:

The Healing Experience

Tears are essential to help you see clearly and maintain the health of your eyes. They can also help communicate your emotions. Your body makes three types of tears. Basal tears are in your eyes all the time to lubricate, nourish and protect your cornea. Basal tears act as a constant shield between the eye and the rest of the world, keeping dirt and debris away. Reflex tears are formed when your eyes need to wash away harmful irritants, such as smoke, foreign bodies or onion fumes. Emotional tears are produced in response to joy, sadness, fear and other emotional states.
(https://www.aao.org/eye-health/tips-prevention/facts-about-tears)

When it comes to demonstrating the kind of vulnerability that is conducive for an authentic healing experience, our willingness to embrace the element of emotional tears is essential to our healing experience. Remember, one of the hindrances to the healing experience is the internal housing of our hurts. As human beings, we process our pain and once that pain is processed, there must be a response of release. British psychiatrist Henry Maudsley is attributed with this quote: "The sorrows that have no vent in tears may make other organs weep." <https://www.quotes.net/quote/15503>.

Without this emotional expression of crying, there would be no vent or no way to release something that's inside of us that if it remains inside of us, it will imprison us to a state of self-destruction. Now, there are many ways to release the pain or the hurt that we are experiencing, but the key is to make sure that the release results in our restoration and

The Healing Experience

not our further ruining. If the release is healthy, it will initiate the process towards an authentic healing experience. You see, in the life experience of Mary and Martha, they responded to their hurt by releasing blame and disappointment towards Jesus. Now, if Jesus wasn't the fullness of love and compassion as we know Him to be, Jesus could have chosen to respond to their release in a way that would have hindered their healing experience. Can you imagine if we stood in the Lord's place and had to respond to the negative attitude in their approach? If we are honest about it, most of us, if not all of us, would struggle to guarantee that we would have responded well to those who are blaming us and demonstrating disappointment towards us because of the hurt they are experiencing in their lives. Thank God that God is God and not us. Thank God for a level of mercy that factors in our moments of temporary insanity that would give us the audacity to approach God negatively. While the sisters released the hurt that they processed in blame and disappointment, we must be careful to realize that the healing experience that they received was not a result of their methods as much as it was a result of The Lord's mercy. The more effective methodology to result in healing in our lives is to demonstrate vulnerability by releasing hurt healthily. Sometimes, in order to experience healing, you have to be able to express your emotions in a healthy way and that is the benefit of emotional tears. Our tears become the vocalization of our vulnerability that can help initiate the voyage from experiences of hurt to that of healing. If healing is the desired destination, then the journey must begin with healthy forms of communication, even if it's communication by way of crying. While we started the healing experience process with showing God where it hurts, before we can show where the hurt is, there must be some form of communication that will identify the existence of the hurt in the first place. Before people will ever show you where they hurt, they will

The Healing Experience

most likely provide communication that they are hurting. Whether that expression or communication is in their words, their behaviors, or their emotions, there will be some kind of communication. Again, for those of us who are after healing, we want to make sure that within our communication or expression, there is a level of vulnerability that will assist us in experiencing the victorious results of healing in our lives. Tears provide that level of vulnerability. From a universal perspective, tears represent an element of vulnerability that provides emotional communication, even when verbalization is constrained. Even when we may struggle to speak a word, our tears will testify of our woundedness. Let's take it a little further. While releasing tears are helpful demonstrations of vulnerability that are needed to experience healing, it is very important that along with our vulnerability, we demonstrate a level of wisdom as it relates to whom we share our vulnerabilities with. I want to suggest that when healing is the goal, you must be careful to present your vulnerability to the right sources. For me, I believe that the first place our vulnerability must be shared is the presence of our God. Regardless of how difficult, draining and devastating life may become, there are healing experiences that will be conferred upon those who choose to be vulnerable enough to cry in the company of our God. You see, our society today has devalued, desensitized and disconnected people from the power of healthy vulnerability, particularly in the lives of men. As men, we struggle to demonstrate any kind of vulnerability, especially if it involves the emotional linguistics of our tears. We have bought into the perception that tears communicate weakness when they really can help serve as gateways to wholeness. As a result, we employ defense mechanisms to constrain the emotional communication of crying because we don't want to expose the distorted perception of our weakness in the form of our tears. We want to present the part of us that is full of power. We

The Healing Experience

want to show the side of us that stands in strength. And so, we do whatever is necessary to prevent the kind of vulnerability that is demonstrated clearly through the tears that we shed. As long as we have this kind of understanding or perception of our tears, we will always struggle to experience the real power of vulnerability, particularly when the vulnerability is expressed or communicated in a healthy way. Let's take a look at an example of the power of vulnerability when communicated through the emotional language of our tears. In Luke 7:11-15, we find a powerful healing experience that was birthed out of the womb of a woman's vulnerability as she communicated her hurt with the emotional language of her tears:

> *11 Soon afterward, Jesus went to a town called Nain, and his disciples and a large crowd went along with him. 12 As he approached the town gate, a dead person was being carried out--the only son of his mother, and she was a widow. And a large crowd from the town was with her. 13 When the Lord saw her, his heart went out to her and he said, "Don't cry." 14 Then he went up and touched the coffin, and those carrying it stood still. He said, "Young man, I say to you, get up!" 15 The dead man sat up and began to talk, and Jesus gave him back to his mother. ~ Luke 7:11-15 (NIV)*

In this experience, we find a woman who is in the midst of her own hurting experience. The Bible identifies her as both a mother and a widow. What is significant about these titles that she is given is that it helps to paint the picture of her pain. It helps to highlight the level of hurt she is experiencing. She is a mother who is burying her son and this comes after she has already become a widow, who has already buried her husband. All of the men in her life were gone. Not only did she lose her husband, but now she loses her son, which also means, her worth has been wounded and weakened by their death. This woman is experiencing extreme hurt that requires an extreme experience of healing in order for her to experience a life of victory beyond these hurting experiences. There she was, experiencing the hurt of having to lay her son to rest and in response to her hurt, the woman engages the power of vulnerability through the expression of her tears. While she is going through her experience, Jesus steps into the scene of her suffering and begins the process of providing this woman with a powerful healing experience. It is important to note, that while Jesus provides the healing experience, it is the power of her vulnerability as expressed by the emotional language of her tears that positions her to experience the provision of The Lord's healing in her life. Let's dive further into this healing experience, so we can see how this woman's vulnerability helped set up the results of victory in her life. When healing is what you are after, you have to be willing to stand in the power of your personal vulnerability because your vulnerability will be critical to experiencing the victorious results of healing in your life.

A. Capturing God's Concentration

In life, there are certain factors that I believe God will take notice of; certain actions or behaviors that will simply capture God's concentration. One major way to capture God's concentration is through the expression of faith. Faith will cause God to focus on the one who is expressing faith in Him. Another way to get God to concentrate on us is by engaging in a life of sin, whether it is infidelity, idolatry, injustice, inequality, etc. Living a life of sin will cause God to

The Healing Experience

focus on you, even if it's to simply help get you back on track with Him. Another way to capture God's concentration is with the healthy expression of our vulnerability as demonstrated in the life experience of this woman in Luke 7. While she was expressing her vulnerability using her tears, in verse 13, the Bible says that Jesus saw her. This is so powerful. She is hurting and Jesus sees her. The emphasis here is that Jesus took notice of her; Jesus' gaze is fixated on this woman. What I find fascinating about Jesus seeing her is that, what Jesus saw was not based on His discernment, even though we know Jesus could easily discern that she was hurting. It was not based on Jesus utilizing some prophetic gift that gave him revelation that she was hurting. Jesus was able to see this woman, he took notice of her, and he fixed his eyes on her because she engaged in the power of vulnerability. That by itself teaches us this principle. Our visibility will increase in value when we express our vulnerability for God to view. In other words, when we engage in the emotional expression of our vulnerability, particularly in a way that we intentionally allow God to view it, God will begin to see us in a way that compels God to concentrate on us. When you read verse 13 of this scripture reference, Jesus reveals the expressive element that caused Him to see her. Let's read verse 13 again. It says, *13 "When the Lord saw her, his heart went out to her and he said, "Don't cry."* This woman processed her pain on the platform of public presentation and in doing so, when she released the pain that she processed, she presented a level of vulnerability with the expression of her tears that would set her up to experience victory in the form of a healing experience.

    The implication is that there is a direct correlation between our vulnerability and our victory. If we want to experience victorious results, we have to be willing to engage in vulnerable responses. Jesus was able to provide this woman a healing experience because she

The Healing Experience

captured His concentration with her vulnerability that was presented in the form of her tears. Similarly, our willingness to demonstrate vulnerability before God can capture God's concentration. Now, notice that when the woman cries, Jesus is there. Jesus is in her area. What that means is, when healing is the goal, if we can position ourselves in His presence while presenting the emotional expression of our pain, God will assign great focus to our lives. He sees her, which also means that He's positioned close enough to her to see her. Conversely, if Jesus is positioned close enough to see her, that also means she is positioned close enough to His presence for Him to be able to notice her pain. Crying on its own merit would not have helped her experience the kind of healing that Jesus was going to provide. What made the difference was that she cried in the company of Christ. What captured the concentration of Christ is that this woman was vulnerable while Christ was in the vicinity. His presence is what made the difference as it relates to the healing she would experience from Jesus. Jesus saw her crying. He was in her presence, which means, when she was crying, she shared her vulnerability with the One person who was able to actually help her heal. When healing is needed, it matters with whom we share our vulnerability. We must be willing to give God access to our vulnerability, not simply because He loves us, but because His presence is pivotal to the experience of healing that is needed in our lives. While being vulnerable is powerful in and out of itself, being vulnerable in the presence of the right people will make the difference. When we are hurting and we desire healing, it is important that we intentionally demonstrate vulnerability in the presence of those with the potential and power to help us prevail over our pain. Whether we demonstrate vulnerability with a counselor, a pastor, our spouse or close friends, the right support system will work to respond to our vulnerability in ways that will connect us to the

The Healing Experience

healing experiences that we need in our lives. If you are experiencing any form of hurt and you desire to heal, consider demonstrating vulnerability in God's presence, particularly using the expression of tears. In Ecclesiastes, the Bible clearly teaches that there is a time to laugh and a time to cry. While the presence of God deserves our worship, God also desires our weeping. As a matter of fact, weeping is a form of worship because the essence of worship is vulnerability by way of intimacy and one of the best ways to produce intimacy with God is being vulnerable enough to cry in His presence. You see, the emotional expression of vulnerability develops intimacy. Whenever our intimacy is involved, it becomes an indicator that causes God's love to identify who is in need of God's concentration. I can't emphasize enough how important it is to engage that kind of intimacy where our vulnerability is free to be expressed. Here's why it makes sense to just be vulnerable and cry before the Lord; God already knows what you've been through and what you're going through so there's a certain response He expects, which is why God constructed us with the capacity for crying. When we choose to refrain from demonstrating our vulnerability, particularly with our tears, we will find ourselves experiencing the effects of lingering bitterness, anger and depression. Our behaviors will reflect our bitterness and our brokenness, simply because we have shut the vent of our tears, and our emotions that should be released have dried up inside of us to the degree that we're contaminated with cries that we've confined within ourselves. As a result, many people remain bitter and broken when God wants to make them better, but in order for God to make them better, God wants them to break down what has dried up and begin to release the cries that were meant to carry out the emotions of hurt that were never meant to stay in their lives. Sometimes, we have to learn to just cry it out before God. Sometimes, we just need to get in an

The Healing Experience

atmosphere or create an atmosphere, where God's presence can manifest and in that atmosphere, just begin to release tears that will capture God's concentration so you can be positioned for the manifestation of the healing experience in your life. At this point, I hope you can see the value of your vulnerability, particularly when expressed through the emotional language of tears. Your tears, when expressed to God and even to the right support system, can lead you to victorious results of healing. Consider the Psalmist who declared in Psalm 34:15 (NIV), *The eyes of the Lord are on the righteous, and his ears are attentive to their cry.* Consider Genesis 21:17-18 (NIV); there the bible gives us this perspective of the power of our vulnerability in the form of our tears: *17 God heard the boy crying, and the angel of God called to Hagar from heaven and said to her, "What is the matter, Hagar? Do not be afraid; God has heard the boy crying as he lies there. 18 Lift the boy up and take him by the hand, for I will make him into a great nation."* Finally, consider the experience of King Hezekiah in 2 Kings 20. God gives the prophetic word that Hezekiah is about to die.

When Hezekiah receives the word, he responds by praying and crying before God's presence and as a result God responds like this in verse 4 and 5: *4 Before Isaiah had left the middle court, the word of the Lord came to him: 5"Go back and tell Hezekiah, the ruler of my people, 'This is what the Lord, the God of your father David, says: I have heard your prayer and seen your tears; I will heal you.* In all of these examples, the common element is the expression of tears that captured God's concentration for the good of those who were vulnerable enough to cry in God's presence.

B. Connecting to God's Compassion

When we are able to express our vulnerability to God, particularly with our tears, not only are we able to capture God's concentration and the concentration of the right support systems, but we are also able to connect to God's compassion for us. Look at vs. 13 again; the text says, 13 When the Lord saw her, His **HEART** went out to her and He said, "Don't cry." Let's deal with this heart matter. His heart went out to her. This verse becomes a powerful presentation of the potential impact of our vulnerability demonstrated through the tears we shed in God's presence. Think about this; our tears are so impactful and so influential that they help to stir up God's compassion towards us. Our tears can help shift God's heart towards a position that causes God to work in favor of our victory. When Jesus saw her weeping, it moved His heart for her and towards her. She was able to connect to the compassion of Christ. If we are serious about experiencing healing in our lives, it becomes important that we demonstrate the level of vulnerability that will connect us to God's compassion for the hurts that we may be experiencing. If you are experiencing hurt in your life, I want you to know that God has an amazing heart for your hurts. God is not one who is cold and callous towards our pain and suffering. God cares and is full of compassion. This is a critical principle to grasp, because until we can truly understand God's compassion towards the hurting, we will always struggle to understand God's commitment towards our healing. God is committed to us experiencing His compassion to help us heal from our hurts. Can I encourage you in this revelation? If you are reading this, please understand that God wants you to experience His heart for your hurts; His heart for your pain; His heart for your losses; His heart for how you've been betrayed; His heart for how you've been mistreated; His heart for how you were

The Healing Experience

traumatized and victimized. God is ready for us to experience His heart going out to us in our hurting experiences, but in order to experience the power of God's compassion that is committed to our healing, we have to plug into that power source with the emotional expressions of our vulnerability. When we really grasp how compassionate God is for the hurting, how can it be that we live in a world where God's children, who have experienced the compassion of God, can be so compassionless towards the hurting, whom God is so compassionate about? How can those who claim they are children of God and they love God have so little compassion towards those who are being traumatized and victimized within our society and our world? How can we have so little compassion for young, black men and women, who are dying to violent actions within their community and dying to unjust, racially-desensitized violence within society? How can we have so little compassion for those whose lives are being ruined by a criminal justice system that advertises rehabilitation, but actualizes greater repression in the lives of so many; How can we have so little compassion for those who are hurting from impoverished conditions. It amazes me how compassionless we can be towards those who are hurting, as though we are not beneficiaries of God's compassion towards our own hurting experiences. If we want to see healing experiences break out in our communities and our societies, then we who represent the God who is full of compassion, we must become agents of compassion in a world full of hurt. This is what Jesus demonstrated in His encounter with this woman. He sees her and His heart goes out to her. His compassion is compelled to work in her favor because of the tears that she was willing to cry. Notice with this mother and widow in the biblical experience, that her tears were shed in public. She does not constrain her cries because people would see her in her vulnerability. You see, while it is important who we share our vulnerability with, there does come a time

The Healing Experience

when the expression of our vulnerability must be courageous enough to present itself when God's presence is present even if it means that our vulnerability will be exposed to the presence of the wrong people. There are times when we may have to make a choice to be vulnerable even in public, especially if it means that the results of our vulnerability will initiate connectivity to God's compassion for our hurting experiences. In other words, if God's presence is present, regardless of who else may be present, we should not allow the presence of people to cause us to miss out on connecting to God's compassion for us. You see, sometimes, we miss out on the compassion of the Father because we are too concerned about the cares of the crowd. When you are after experiences of healing from God, then you have to find a way to connect to God's compassion regardless of the crowd that may witness your moment of weakness. Be careful of not allowing yourself to get sidetracked by those who are standing in your space. If God is in your space, then let your suffering speak. You have to be willing to be vulnerable in God's presence, so that you can connect to God's compassion that will set you up to experience victorious conclusions of a healing experience. When we truly start connecting to God's compassion with our cries, when we truly begin to tap into the power of our vulnerability that is able to move God's heart, then God will begin to deal with our hurts. It doesn't even matter if we were the cause of our own hurts; when we learn to touch God's heart with our tears, God's compassion will begin the process of breaking the chains of our hurts. If you are going through your own hurting experiences, I challenge you to trust God with your tears. I decree a level of grace to allow God to see your real face that has been going through the hurting experiences. Even while you're reading this book, I challenge you to open the vault of vulnerability and allow your vulnerability to become visible and voice itself through the emotional expression of your tears;

give yourself permission to cry in God's presence and in the presence of those whom God may strategically position in your life to help you experience victorious results of healing in your life.

C. Communicating with God's Comfort

As we continue in the process of trying to find victory in our vulnerability, what will assist us greatly in trying to experience the victorious results of a healing experience is learning to allow our tears to communicate with God's desire to comfort us when we are hurting. The revelation that we must grab a hold of and maintain our grip on, is that the same God who is committed to being compassionate, is also committed to providing comfort to those who hurt. God is so committed to providing comfort for our hurting experiences, that God would make it a part of His plan for humanity to invest and indwell The Holy Spirit in us, the same Holy Spirit whom Jesus identifies as The Comforter. Whenever we are experiencing hurt, particularly those of us who are children of God, we can rest assured that the love and compassion of our heavenly Father moves Him towards providing comfort. The Apostle Paul reminds us of God's desire and determination as it relates to providing comfort to those of us who are experiencing hurt. In his letter to the church of Corinth, Paul writes this: *3 Praise be to the God and Father of our Lord Jesus Christ, the Father of compassion and the God of all comfort, 4 who comforts us in all our troubles, so that we can comfort those in any trouble with the comfort we ourselves receive from God* (2 Corinthians 1:3-4 New International Version). Now, if we are to experience this comfort that God desires and is determined to provide, it is important that we learn how to communicate in such a way that we are able to pierce the sensitivity of

The Healing Experience

God's compassion by allowing our tears to make the appeal. The power of your tears is that it becomes a form of communication that appeals to God's compassion and comfort. Let's go back to the life experience of this mother and widow in Luke 7 so we can see this communication that taps into the compassion of Christ, which moves Him to providing comfort as part of her healing experience. In vs 13, the bible says, *13 When the Lord saw her, his heart went out to her and he said, "Don't cry."* The moment Jesus sees her, particularly in the expression of her vulnerability, His compassion moves Him towards comforting her. At this point, the communication has begun. The woman begins the communication process with the non-verbal emotional expression of her tears. Jesus responds to her communication with powerful words. He approaches the woman and tells her not to cry. When we learn to be vulnerable with our tears before the Lord, when we learn to weep in His presence, we can create opportunities for God to communicate words of comfort into our lives. Now, notice the words of Comfort that she receives. Jesus says to her, "Don't cry", which seems unrealistic and uncompassionate for someone who is full of compassion and comfort. To understand the Lord's approach in providing comfort, you have to view the approach from the angle and the agenda of the healing experience. When Jesus tells her don't cry, he's not saying it because He's against her crying, but rather, it's a word of comfort to help shift her from crying. When healing is the agenda, while we may start in tears, while we may start in emotional despair, God's desire and determination to comfort won't let us stay in that state without seeking to shift us from that state. In other words, when God seeks to comfort us as part of His healing experience for us, God will provide words to shift us from weeping, so that our lives are not restricted and bound to our weeping. While God wants us to be vulnerable with our tears, the purpose of our vulnerability is to help

The Healing Experience

transition us into results of victory. You see, sometimes, if we are not careful, we will find ourselves substituting the need to be comforted with a desire to be coddled. Being comforted can set you up for healing; being coddled can keep you suppressed in your hurt. The motive for both may be the same, but the results will often differ. People who are coddled can become crippled to their conditions. Coddling can result in conclusions of conditional complacency. Sometimes, the hurt can be so challenging and so crushing to us that we will allow the hurt to control us to the degree that even when we cry, our cries that should be vehicles of comfort and healing end up being nothing more than a distorted pattern of reliving and residing in our pain. As a result, when we are going through hurt, we have to be careful of the kind of help that we are receiving. If healing is the goal, then we can't afford to be coddled, but we must be properly comforted. This is where God demonstrates His capacity as the ultimate strategist. Even though we may want to be coddled, God will look beyond what we want in order to give us what will work. Because God knows coddling won't work towards healing, God will provide the kind of comfort that is conducive to our healing. When Jesus tells the woman not to cry, He wasn't dismissing the hurt she was experiencing; but rather, He was setting her up to shift from the state of hurt so that healing would not be hindered. Sometimes, in order for healing to be dispensed, hurt must be disrupted from maintaining its effect on our mind and our behavior. We will always struggle to experience healing if we don't find a way to interrupt the way our hurts continue to dominate our lives. As a result, when we engage in healthy conversations with God where our tears are allowed to communicate our hurt, God's comfort will begin to communicate back to us in ways that will interrupt the new norm created by our hurts. Once the new norm has been disrupted by God's means of providing comfort, God then is able to provide contributions beyond our human capacity to ensure that the vulnerability we shared with Him leads to the victorious results that He wants us to have, in the form of our healing experience.

A. Creating the Case for God's Contribution

Hopefully by now, we should have a pretty good idea of how important the emotional expression of our vulnerability is when it comes to leading us to victorious results in our lives. Before we close this particular chapter, I would like to offer one more important way that our vulnerability can help us experience victorious results of healing in our lives. Not only does our emotional expression, and in this particular woman's experience, the emotional expression of tears give us the capacity to Capture God's Concentration, to connect to God's compassion and to communicate with God's comfort, but our tears can also create the case for God to make heavenly contributions to help us experience victory in the form of healing. I've discovered that there are certain aspects of healing that are heavily dependent on divine contributions. While God has allowed the intelligence of humanity to develop many ways to help bring healing into someone's life, while we have mental health professionals and spiritual counselors and healing ministers who are able to assist in helping people experience measures of healing in their lives, the reality is, there are levels of healing that will only be experienced by way of direct contribution from God. This divine contribution is initiated by the intimacy of our vulnerability. When we are able to invest our vulnerability in God's presence, our investment will initiate God's involvement to address whatever issue has caused us to shed our tears. Let's look at the woman's experience in Luke 7. She is funeralizing her son and while they are processing

The Healing Experience

forward, the woman completely lets her guard down and is operating at a very vulnerable state. As she is crying, Jesus sees her, tells her not to cry and then makes a contribution to help bring about the healing conclusion that He wanted her to experience. In verse 14, the bible says this: *14 Then he went up and touched the coffin, and those carrying it stood still. He said, "Young man, I say to you, get up!"* This mother has now reached the point in the process of experiencing her healing where Jesus has to get involved and intervene to make this healing experience effective in her life. Remember, she has already lost her husband and now her son. For that culture, not being connected to a man was a big deal. The healing that she needed couldn't happen in her life without Jesus making direct contributions. Knowing this, Jesus touches the coffin; He touches the places or the thing in her life that has caused her to hurt and show her vulnerability in the tears that she cried. This contribution by Jesus is directly correlated to her willingness to cry regardless of the crowd around her. That's powerful because that tells me, when we learn to give God the emotional expression of our vulnerability, God's love will not be able to stay on the sidelines while our tears are being shed. When tears are shed as an emotional expression of our vulnerability, those tears become an indication of our personal invitation for God to get involved with His personal intervention. When Jesus saw her and the tears she shed, the tears communicated the need for divine contribution. Jesus responds by touching the coffin. Notice what happens when He does; according to the story, the pallbearers stood still. These people were assigned to carry and bury her son. You see, when we are after a healing experience that only God can provide, we have to realize there are people in our lives whom the enemy may try to use to help maintain the results of the hurt that we have experienced. And sometimes, it's not even the enemy; sometimes, people who love us can participate in the

The Healing Experience

sabotage of our healing experience, simply because they don't have the kind of faith that can expect God to turn things around in your life. Sometimes, the hurt we experience can be so devastating that people just don't see how we can recover from it. And so, instead of trying to help us heal, they help us manage. They help us learn to live in the new normal of our hurt. They don't see any other alternative that they can provide to address the hurt, so they simply settle with the reality that there is no help for this kind of hurt. This is where divine contribution is so critical to our healing experience. You see, unlike with Lazarus, whom Jesus told the crowd to loose him and let him go, in this situation, Jesus did not use the help of those in her space. Jesus shut down their help because the only thing they knew how to do was carry and bury stuff; they were good at carrying people who have died; they were good at carrying people who were lifeless, unproductive in life. In carrying them, they become crutches that continue the crippling conditions that they are in. Some people can't get healed because too many people are trying to carry those who hurt and when you carry people, you end up coddling people and the coddling further maintains the hurting condition that they are in. Not only were the pallbearers good at carrying, but they were also good at burying. In other words, they knew what to do to keep you stuck in your hurting place. Some people are just good at keeping you in the space of your suffering. They know how to keep you living in your hurt. And so, when trying to heal, we have to be careful of who we are allowing into sensitive areas of your life. Be careful of receiving support from people who only know how to be negative; who only know how to speak death into your life; be careful of people who only report bad news and only tell you what you can't do and what God won't do in your life. And so, in making contributions, God has to put a stop to the support that is only sabotaging the success of the healing experience. Even people with the

The Healing Experience

best intentions can stand in the way of divine intervention. As a result, when healing is the goal, sometimes, God will have to contribute to the cause of healing by causing people who don't know how to bless you in your brokenness to stand still while He works on your brokenness to bring about your blessing. While trying to heal, don't be surprised if some people just stop trying to help you. Don't get upset and offended by some people who see you suffering but just stand on the sidelines. It may be a part of God's contribution to block them from helping you because their help would only hurt you even further. Sometimes, part of God's involvement is interrupting who we allow to work on our behalf. Notice that Jesus was not able to deal with the Son, who was the source of this woman's hurt, until the pallbearers stopped helping. The moment they stopped, the healing experience went into full effect. Sometimes, we have to simply come to the resolution that there are some healing experiences that are just beyond our capacity. We can try therapy, we can try medicine, we can try to decree and declare our healing, but at the end of the day, there are some measures of healing that God will have to contribute and to get that contribution, we must be willing to engage in an exchange of our weeping for his healing works; our sorrows for His joy; our vulnerability for His victory. I want to end this chapter with a testimony from the life of Jacob and Rachel. Even though they experienced levels of hurt prior to getting married, which eventually opened the door to more hurt during their marriage, I am thrilled to be able to report that they are still married and their marriage is not only surviving, but thriving. They are not simply enduring each other, but they are actually enjoying each other. While I'm sure there are more levels of healing for them to reach, the healing that they have already experienced is undeniable. What is the evidence of their healing you may be asking? Prior to their healing experience, Jacob and Rachel would publicly present a productive, prosperous and

The Healing Experience

pleasurable partnership while privately, their partnership was being paralyzed by their pain that wasn't being properly addressed. Prior to their healing, they were imbalanced in the involvement that they invested in their career, church and community. If you observe their relationship now, what you will see is a couple operating with measures of healing that empowers them to operate in transparency towards one another and even towards the public. They are no longer trying to put on a show to impress anyone. They are more intentional about recognizing their hurts and the hurt they may be causing one another. They are more understanding and compassionate towards one another. They have become more intentional about balancing their investment of personal involvement in various areas of their lives. They are no longer hostages to their hurt. While they almost didn't make it, their willingness to address their hurt and give God access to their hurt allowed God the opportunity to contribute to their healing with His personal involvement. In addition to the counseling, in addition to having the right support system around them, in addition to all of the resources that may have assisted in the measure of healing that they have and continue to experience, I believe without question that God's contribution of His personal involvement was absolutely mandatory to their healing. If you were to speak to them now, what has become obvious at least to me is that they are living much better now than the presentation of life they had while they were still being held hostage to their hurts. Part of the power of their healing experience is that their healing helped them to see that all of their hurt was not terminal. Healing helped them to see and now live in the reality, that when hurt is addressed and God has access to it, what could have been terminal can be very transitional. I believe Jacob and Rachel's healing experience is an example of what God is able and willing to do for all of us who are in need of healing. As we make healing a necessary part of our lives,

The Healing Experience

we will continue to transition towards pursuits and positions of God's greater plans and purposes for our lives.

The Healing Experience

The Healing Experience Notes:

___

___

___

___

___

___

___

___

___

___

___

___

___

___

___

___

___

CHAPTER THREE

MORE LEVELS OF LIFE TO LIVE

One day, I was given the heartbreaking news that Abram and Sarai (not their actual names), an amazing couple whom I have grown to know and love, have gone through with the process of divorce. By the time I discovered the news, both individuals had moved on trying to live in the aftermath of their divorce. I was able to have brief communication with both and what I discovered that was true for both was that the devastation of divorce was not the demise of their destiny. While they both struggled and suffered with the process in their own way, after going through it, they also discovered that their lives did not end simply because their marriage did. If they were to testify to the emotional and holistic condition of their lives today, based on the communication that I had with each of them, I am confident that they both would say that while they were hurting because their marriage failed, they found a measure of healing in being in a relationship with the God who loves them and is not yet finished with either of them. While it seemed like life was over for them, particularly for Sarai, while it seemed like her world was coming to an end, while life crashed down on her, Sarai began and continues to rely on a level of

The Healing Experience

hope in God that she has made bigger than the hurt of divorce. Her hope in God gives her the expectation that God must have more life for her to live beyond the level of hurt that she had experienced. You see, when God provides a healing experience for your life, within the makeup of God's healing, there is the production of hope. This level of hope is powerful because if it is received, it can free one from the prisons that hurt can create in our lives. Again, the hope that healing will produce is that life does not end on the level of our hurts, but on the other side of that hurtful experience, God has more levels of life that His purpose is waiting for us to live. You see, no matter what we have gone through in our lives, regardless of how turbulent, troublesome or even traumatic the tribulations, God's healing experience is able to trump the turbulence, troubles and trauma of our trials that may have the potential to trap us from experiencing the territory of triumph into which God has already planned to transition us. This is part of the power and the purpose of The Healing Experience. God establishes the power of Healing, so that our lives don't end at the place of our hurt, but transitions us towards new beginnings that God will usher us into after the experiences that left us hurting. The Healing experience is evidence that God does not give our history nor does God give our current reality the authority to keep us from our greater destiny. What that means for us is that even the worst of what we have gone through and may still be going through, every hurting experience must submit and surrender to God's plan to save us from being stifled and suppressed by the hurt. This concept is powerful and one of the reasons why I believe it is so necessary that we engage this process of experiencing God's healing that He has reserved for us.

Now, while trying to engage this level of healing that is going to take us to new levels of life, we have to be careful to guard against

The Healing Experience

anything that would try to hinder us from experiencing the hope that healing produces. When healing is the agenda, we have to understand that there is warfare at work to keep us prisoners of our wounds. There is a war against our mind and a war happening in our mind to keep us from living beyond the levels of our hurt. We have to be on guard, particularly, in our mind, because the mind becomes the battleground that births bondage or breakthrough. I believe that one of the reasons healing can be very difficult for some people to experience is because oftentimes, the severity of the hurt has taken captive the space in our mind. As a result, because of the state of our mind, we can sometimes find ourselves being stuck from engaging in what matters in our lives. In other words, because the experiences we have gone through were so devastating, those experiences begin to dominate our lives by detaining us to the memory of what damaged us. This is the warfare strategy at work. Damage any progressive motion by detaining one to a past memory. What is interesting about this strategy is that, even positive memories can detain us and end up damaging our progressive motion. This understanding is a critical element to the concept of tradition. Traditions are established based on a positive memory of an experience that one has deemed is worth repetition. The challenge with these positive memories is that we can get so attached to them that it prevents us from trying something different or new that may yield better results. This is what many institutions struggle with. Whether it's a business, a church, or a non-profit organization, sometimes, the positive memory becomes a tradition that traps the organization from necessary trying new tactics or transitioning into new territories that may be different from their norm.

    This was seemingly the result of organizations like Blockbuster because they were too attached to the past memory of their successful business strategy. As a result, when it was time to transition and try

The Healing Experience

new tactics, they could not get past the memories of how successful their strategies have been and that damaged the progressive motion that was necessary for future success. So even positive memories can damage progression if we get detained by them. But while positive memories can keep us from experiencing life beyond the level of hurting experiences, nothing detains us more from making progress to new levels of life like the memories of our hurts. Sometimes, the tribulations that we've gone through were so traumatic and because of how traumatic they were, we find ourselves living our lives in the present being tormented by the trauma even though we may no longer be trapped in the tribulation that traumatized us. And so what happens is, oftentimes, we are hurting even though what caused our hurt is no longer a threat to us, but because of the initial experience, and for many people, experiences after experiences, our lives are now consumed by the memory of it to such a degree that the memory has a chokehold on our destiny. The memory has become a monument that is minimizing our movements toward God's greater mission for our lives. The memory ends up seemingly preventing us from living the life of destiny that God says He has in store for us even after all of the experiences that hurt us. And so, we have to guard against being detained by our memories because if our memories continue to dominate our lives, the door will be opened for the spirit of oppression to overwhelm our opportunities. When you live in and under oppression, even the most obvious of opportunities will be observed as obstacles and opposition. To help us better understand this concept of how our hurts can keep us from progressing to greater levels of life beyond the level of hurt, let's take a look at the healing experience that the biblical character Job received in his life. In the first 2 chapters of the book of Job, Job has several extreme traumatic experiences. If you have experienced trauma in your life, you will notice that traumatic

The Healing Experience

experiences have the potential to either turn you towards God or it can turn you away from God. For Job, his trauma turned him towards God. In response to his trauma, Job praised God in spite of his predicaments. He provides one of the most memorable praise responses when he declared that *The Lord gives, and the Lord takes away; blessed be the name of the Lord.* While that response is appropriate and impressive, Job's response was only temporary because it only lasted for the first 2 chapters of his life's story. While he started off with praise and worship, the reality is, the trauma of what he went through began to consume his life. The evidence of his oppression is found in chapters 3-38, where Job engages in conversation with His friends that breaks His concentration off of God and that's never a good idea. For about 35 chapters, Job seems to be operating in the oppression of his experience as he continues the back and forth with his friends. Evidence of oppression is when the memories of our wounds become monuments in our world. You know your memory is a monument when it dominates every area of your life. Even Job's relationships were being centered on the hurting experience that Job had gone through and was still going through. In his hurt, Job became consumed with debates and arguments with his friends to show off his innocence and self-righteousness, instead of God's sovereignty. He couldn't get past the fact that he didn't deserve to suffer because of how good he was. It was all about him, his righteousness; He became right while everybody, including God, became wrong. This was the impact of His wounds. When wounds are oppressing us, it will influence us to do whatever we can to protect ourselves at all costs, even if it puts us at odds with God. When you are oppressed by your wounds, you begin to make observations through the outlook of your wounds. So now, you look at everybody as an enemy, including God. Everybody is wrong including God.

Oppression makes you defensive against and suspicious of everyone including God. This is the kind of impact oppression was having on Job's life. Throughout various moments in my ministry, I have seen the impact of oppression on the lives of many, including my own. I noticed myself becoming cautious of different people in ministry because I was seeing them through the lens of previous ministry experiences that were oppressing my functionality in the current ministry. Like Job, I needed a healing experience to break the oppression that hurt had created in my life. If I was going to continue in ministry in a healthy and effective way, I could no longer continue in my oppression, but I needed a healing experience to break the oppression of hurt off of my life. I needed to heal from it so I could experience the levels of life that God had for me and my ministry beyond the levels of hurt that I had experienced and to which I was seemingly being held hostage. There were more levels of life for me to live, but I needed healing to help me overcome the oppression that was keeping me prisoner to the levels of pain that I had already experienced.

A. Operate On the Oppression

To experience healing from the oppression that was holding me hostage to the levels of hurt that I had experienced in my ministry, I had to grow to a place of maturity that allowed God to operate on the oppression in my life. This principle became clear to me when I observed the story of Job's healing experience. You see, after allowing Job to engage in an extensive moment of self-defense, which ends up extending the experience of his hurt, God interrupts Job with 4 chapters worth of tongue-lashing found in Job 38 through Job 41. This

The Healing Experience

tongue lashing eventually leads us to the details of Job's healing experience. Let's look at the end of Job's story and there we will find the process of Job's healing experience:

> *7 After the Lord had finished speaking to Job, he said to Eliphaz, "I am angry with you and your two friends, because you did not speak the truth about me, the way my servant Job did. 8 Now take seven bulls and seven rams to Job and offer them as a sacrifice for yourselves. Job will pray for you, and I will answer his prayer and not disgrace you the way you deserve. You did not speak the truth about me as he did." 9 Eliphaz, Bildad, and Zophar did what the Lord had told them to do, and the Lord answered Job's prayer. 10 Then, after Job had prayed for his three friends, the Lord made him prosperous again and gave him twice as much as he had had before. 11 All Job's brothers and sisters and former friends came to visit him and feasted with him in his house. They expressed their sympathy and comforted him for all the troubles the Lord had brought on him. Each of them gave him some money and a gold ring. 12 The Lord blessed the last part of Job's life even more than he had blessed the first. Job owned fourteen thousand sheep, six thousand camels, two thousand head of cattle, and one thousand donkeys. (Job 42:7-12 GNT)*

The Healing Experience

Let's look at the first part of verse 7 again. The text says, *7 After the LORD had finished speaking to Job*...What we see here is that God had a moment of depositing words into Job's life. God speaks words to operate on His wounds so He can break Job free from the oppression of his wounds. Once God spoke to him, once he received words from God, the process of healing began. You see, until we are willing to let God's word speak concerning our wounds, we will never break free from the oppression of our wounds. Now, when you look at the Word of the Lord to Job concerning the hurt He was being controlled or influenced by, God's word was fluffy, firm. It wasn't a gentle word. It was a word that would be considered tough love by many. As a matter of fact, if God engaged some of us in this manner, we would probably respond with great offense. But this was God's approach to Job. God gave Job a tongue lashing of a lifetime because Job would dare put himself on God's level or even above God. Job would dare consider himself righteous which means what God has allowed decreased God's ability to be right in Job's life. So God begins speaking and the words immediately address the wounds of Job's life. Sometimes, when we are dealing with wounds from even the most severe situations, one of the most necessary elements to assist in ensuring an authentic healing experience is to allow God's word to operate on our wounds. I am a firm believer that in order to break free from the oppression of our wounds, God must be given the freedom to apply the spiritual procedure of His word over our wounds, which means, the one who is oppressed must be open to God's surgical operation. God's word must be given freedom to perform surgery on the hurts that are holding us hostage. This kind of heavenly surgery is going to require the oppressed to uncover the bandages that block our wounds so that God's word can have direct contact with the wound. Now, this process isn't always comfortable nor convenient. You see,

The Healing Experience

in order for this surgical process to be effective, the one who is dealing with the oppression of their wounds must submit and surrender themselves to the instructions and the implementation of whatever God's word may diagnose and prescribe concerning the hurts and disappointments and the trauma that may be oppressing us. The more we allow God to apply His word over the wound, the more healing we will see the wound experiencing. Let's take it a little deeper. Like any surgical procedure, there are always challenges, particularly in the recovery process. The more severe the wound, the more we will be stretched by the operation and the subsequent recovery process. Similarly, when God's word is performing surgery on our wounds, it comes with some stretching challenges for us. What makes this challenging is that sometimes, the surgical process or procedures of God's word will result in our healing experience by first hurting our expectations. Sometimes, when we go to God's word or when we hear God's word, we expect God to minister in a way that makes us comfortable and makes us feel good, but sometimes, God's word will hurt before it heals. Sometimes, God's word will step on your toes in order to heal your whole body. Sometimes, God has to deal with us internally; God will sometimes show us our personal issues and bring insight as it relates to what is going on inside of us and how what is going on in us internally may have the kind of impact that is allowing our wounds to oppress us even though it should have no authority over us.

You see for Job, the oppression showed up in the content of his conversation with his friends. The internal issue or infection that God had to give Job insight into was his ego and his ego was extending the oppression that evolved from his hurting experience. You see, when Job's friends began to accuse him of doing wrong, his ego became bothered to the degree that he had to express confidence in his own

The Healing Experience

righteousness. His oppression caused his ego to rise to the surface and build a defense case, not only against his friends, but also against God. In building that defense through debates and arguments, Job found himself operating as a prisoner to oppression. As a result, when God's word goes to operate on Job's oppression in Job chapters 38-41, God speaks words that deal with the infection of his ego. In essence, God seemingly begins to tell Job that he has gotten beside himself. God seems to suggest to Job that he must have forgotten who God is. He begins to remind Job of His divine reputation and resume. God seemingly tells Job to check himself. If we observe the words that God uses to operate on Job's wounds, it is likened to one having surgery performed on his or her wounds. And just like surgery to our physical body, experiencing surgery from God's word can be painful. If the truth be told, it won't always be easy to receive God's Word when it is addressing us internally. Receiving God's word won't always be smooth. Sometimes, the surgical process of God operating on our wounds will be painful because God will deal with areas in us that may be prolonging the oppression that was never meant to keep us in the prison of oppression. Think about most surgical operations; surgery often requires the one who is receiving surgery to be cut by the surgeon. From a spiritual perspective, oppression may require a level of spiritual operation that may be received as offense by the one who is being oppressed. If Job would've kept His concentration on God like He did in chapters 1 and 2, he may not have been oppressed for so many chapters of His life. Because of His ego, he extended the process of his pain. It was something in him that God needed him to see in order to heal him of the hurt that was oppressing him. This is critical to our healing. While many people can experience measures of healing and deliverance from their wounds so that it no longer exists externally, the oppression will often continue to be an obstacle if there

The Healing Experience

is something internally that keeps doors open for the enemy to use the memory of the wound to bring oppression into their lives. What is critical, then, to our healing experience and what I believe God wants to emphasize is the importance of self-examination and self-observation. In other words, when operating on oppression, it is important to wrestle with questions like this: *What is it in me that I may need God to deal with so that I'm no longer a prisoner to my pain? What is it in me that keeps giving authority to past adversities?* Again, let me drill the point that when we go to God's word and we ask God about the oppressions that we're dealing with; when we ask God about overcoming the oppression from being wounded by rape, molestation, betrayal, lies, scandals, rejection, abandonment and various forms of discrimination and injustice; when we ask God's word about these issues, while the operation of God's word may sometimes feel good, there are moments however when God's love may express itself by shining a light on us directly so that we can see what needs to be healed in us that will assist in our breakthrough from the oppression to which our hurts may have exposed us. Here is the truth of the matter: We will not always want to hear what God has to say about what we're going through, but we are going to have to just take it. We are going to have to swallow whatever pill God gives us in order to bring about our healing experience. All of us, on some level, have had experiences where our parents or the doctor would prescribe medicine that just didn't taste good. I can remember my mother bringing me a spoon full of some horrible concoction that she deemed would provide great health benefits to my body. Every year before the school semester would begin, she would get a bottle of what I believe was cod fish oil and give me a spoon full. While I'm not sure of what the health benefits were, I am absolutely sure of the horror I experienced as I would gulp this concoction down. Sometimes, when we want to experience the benefits of God's healing, we have to understand that no matter how bad it may taste, whatever spoonful of scriptural concoctions that God brings before us, we must be submissive enough to drink it so we can experience healing from the oppression that our wounds have created in our lives. We may not always understand it, nor will we always agree with it, but if we want healing, if we want to finally be over it where it no longer impacts our lives, we've got to buckle down and simply go through with the operation of God's word and let God orchestrate healing in our world. You see, it wasn't until after God spoke a word to Job that Job's inner healing began, bringing his ego under subjection, which then opens the door for a full healing experience that would result in levels of life beyond the hurt that was oppressing him. Like Job, we must be open to God's word speaking to us and addressing us inwardly and allow that to open the door for measures of healing that will lead us to greater levels of life beyond our hurt.

B. Don't Get Consumed by Condemnation

When we are trying to experience healing that will lead us to greater levels of life beyond our hurt, while we must be careful to allow God to operate on our wounds, we must also be careful not to allow ourselves to get consumed by those who may be condemning us while we are in process. When we look at Job's healing experience, what I find so alarming is that Job may have actually delayed his healing experience and the greater life God had planned for him beyond the hurt because he became consumed by the condemnation of his friends. Think about this; Job spent about 35 chapters of his life story debating his position and defending himself against his friend's interpretation of his situation. The more he debated and the more he

The Healing Experience

engaged conversations with them about his experiences, the more he would remain consumed by the experiences. It wasn't until God intervened in chapter 38 that Job would be free from being consumed by his friend's opinions of his hurt. What Job didn't understand and what many of us have to understand so that we can move beyond the level of our hurt and embrace greater levels of life is the principle that God demonstrates in Job 42:7. Let's look at the verse again; the text says this: *7 After the Lord had finished speaking to Job, he said to Eliphaz, "I am angry with you and your two friends, because you did not speak the truth about me, the way my servant Job did.* Here is the principle that is paramount to our ability to propel beyond our hurts into new levels of life that God wants us to live out: The same God who is operating on us and our wounds internally, will also be dealing with those who were positioned to comfort us, but persisted in condemning us. When you are trying to heal, you have to be careful of feeding your oppression by feasting on the opinions of others. If you want your oppression to last, keep listening to the opinions of those whose opinions don't line up with God's Word. The opinions can be good or bad, but if they don't line up with God's word, then the opinion can often sustain the oppression. Sometimes, we struggle to heal and move forward, to the life that God has for us after the hurtful experiences because we get consumed by the company that we keep. I can't stress how critical it is to guard yourself against the opinions of people. Sometimes the people who should be comforting us end up doing more to condemn us which does nothing more than keep us contained in our pain. And so because of how they dealt with Job, God gets angry and now has to deal with them. You see, the problem with his friends was, they were men of conventional wisdom, men of tradition and they applied their traditions to Job's tribulation. You see, traditionally, it was believed that one's suffering was the result of

The Healing Experience

one's sin and so because of their tradition, because of this spirit of religion, they ended up taking on the role of Satan and became the accuser of their brother. In chapter 1 and 2, Satan made accusations against Job, and here they are now, accusing Job when they should be assisting Him; they are condemning when they should be comforting. The wrong support system will only help sustain the hurt that is suppressing your shift to life beyond the hurt. Sometimes, when you're going through your worst, it's the people who are closest to you that can do more to condemn you. Sometimes, the people you thought would be the first ones to help you end up doing more to make you a hostage to your hurts. The results of being consumed by people, their thoughts and opinions is that, you will intensify the experience of oppression. The intensity now makes healing even more difficult because I'm already struggling to heal on my own. To now add the ingredient of people who I thought were coming to comfort me, but are crushing me by condemning me, only leaves me deeper in the oppression. Hence, many end up stuck because their support systems were sabotaged. Not only are they dealing with the oppression of their wounds, but now the oppression is intensified because people have added to their hurts. Here's how this impacts our healing experience. When God moves to heal us from the wound, because we became consumed by the condemnation of others, we face the danger of developing grudges and resentment towards the people who added to the hurt when they should've been assisting us past the hurt. While we are no longer dealing with what hurt us, we develop another infection that is triggered by the people to whom we have grudges and resentment against, because they said the wrong things and we consumed it; because they did the wrong things and we consumed it. We go into defense mode, which is survival mode. In survival mode, I have to go on the offense and attack you with my attitude and my words and my behaviors. In survival mode, I live to prove you wrong. In survival mode, my focus is to make you feel bad about how you handled me. I use my words and my behavior to try and make you hurt for the way you handled me because I consumed your condemnation, which only added to the contamination that left me oppressed. If we are serious about experiencing the kind of healing that will lead to greater life beyond the hurt, then we must be careful that while we may get upset with people, while we may experience more hurt by what they say or do, we can't make it our responsibility to make them suffer. If we want healing, we have to keep our focus off what others are saying and doing to condemn us. If not, hurting becomes the main attraction of our lives. Hurting becomes the agenda and that will always get in the way of healing. Here is a powerful revelation for when healing is the goal. Healing will not manifest when hurting is the mission; If we become consumed with hurting people who hurt us, then we can't get healed from what hurt us. In our flesh, we may want them to hurt as much as they made us hurt with their condemnation, but we have to let God fight for us while we maintain our focus on God. When healing is the goal, we can't war from the place of our woundedness, but we must learn to war from the place of our worship, which is the place of maintaining focus on God and the process of healing He is taking us through, so that we can live beyond the levels of hurt and embrace greater levels of life.

C. Use Forgiveness to Finance Freedom

Another powerful principle that is necessary to experience healing that leads to more levels of life beyond our hurt is the principle of forgiveness. When a person is stuck in the space of suffering, when one is being held hostage to hurt, that level of oppression requires the

The Healing Experience

payment of forgiveness to finance the desired level of freedom. This concept is seen in Job's healing experience found in Job 42:10 (GNT). In that verse, the bible says this: *10 After Job had prayed for his friends, the LORD made him prosperous again and gave him twice as much as he had before.* Notice the timing of Job's healing experience. The Lord makes him prosperous again "after" he prayed for his friends. Remember, Job has been arguing with his friends. He has been defending himself against their accusations and judgements. Instead of being comforted by them, he was condemned by them. But, notice that while they may have added to his hurt and while they assisted the oppressive condition that the hurt evolved into, Job's healing experience doesn't manifest until after he prays for them. Job had to transition from arguing with his friends to making an appeal for his friends by way of prayer. This act of prayer becomes the expression of Job willing to exonerate his friends for their contribution towards his oppression. When Job prays for them, he is demonstrating that his heart has moved towards forgiveness for his friends. His forgiveness expressed through his prayer served as the prerequisite for the healing experience. Before there can be true, authentic healing, there must be the expression or the demonstration of authentic, sincere forgiveness that flows from the heart of the person who needs healing. Forgiveness is a critical component to healing. The challenge we have with forgiveness is that often when we are engaging in forgiveness, we limit forgiveness to the words that we release. We will communicate forgiveness with our mouths. We will tell people that we forgive them for what they have done to us. And while verbalizing forgiveness is important, Job's healing experience presents a mature and developed understanding of forgiveness. God uses Job's experience to help stretch our understanding of the kind of forgiveness that is necessary to experience freedom from the prison of oppression that hurt has created

The Healing Experience

in our lives. You see, if we want to be totally free from some things, if we want to get past the hurting experiences that we have gone through so that it no longer has a hold on us, then we must engage in the kind of forgiveness that matures beyond verbalization into verification. In other words, verbalizing forgiveness isn't good enough to get you free from the oppression that hurt may have created in our lives. Forgiveness must be demonstrated. When forgiveness is fully released, it becomes the payment that we make in order to ensure our freedom from the prisons of oppression that our hurts have established in our lives. Sometimes, we can cheapen the value of forgiveness with our words, which then makes the payment insufficient to cover the fee that authentic freedom requires of us. This helps to explain why so many people struggle to experience greater levels of life beyond the levels of hurt they have experienced. Many people simply struggle with the demonstration of forgiveness. Now, here is the key to operating at this level of forgiveness. Notice what God tells Job's friends:

> *7 After the Lord had finished speaking to Job, he said to Eliphaz, "I am angry with you and your two friends, because you did not speak the truth about me, the way my servant Job did. 8 Now take seven bulls and seven rams to Job and offer them as a sacrifice for yourselves. Job will pray for you, and I will answer his prayer and not disgrace you the way you deserve. You did not speak the truth about me as he did." Job 42:7-8 (GNT)*

God tells Job's friends that they are to go to Job with an offering. Job will pray for them and that will cause God to receive and forgive them. What is so powerful about this is, there is no indication that God

The Healing Experience

instructed Job to forgive or that God told Job that he was obligated to forgive them by way of praying for them. This highlights an incredible revelation and that is this: The reason Job was able to pray for them, and in essence forgive them even without God instructing him to or requiring him to, is because Job's healing had already begun when God dealt with him internally. When Job prays, his prayer expresses the power that forgiveness has to continue making payments that would otherwise result in a penalty against the freedom, for which his forgiveness has already begun paying. Because Job was faithful in paying the fee of forgiveness that freedom required, not only did Job get free of oppression, but his friends also experienced freedom from the part they played that assisted Job's state of oppression. Job ends up living in new levels of life because he was financed his freedom with his forgiveness. For those of us who are serious about experiencing the greater levels of life beyond the levels of our hurt, we must understand that until we can faithfully cover the fee of forgiveness, we won't qualify for the kind of freedom that will help us experience greater levels of life beyond our hurts.

    Now, if you're wondering about the fee of forgiveness, here it is: *The fee of forgiveness that will finance freedom is forgiveness that declares and demonstrates that all charges have been cleared.* If I am going to cover that fee, then that means I am declaring and demonstrating that the debts have been completely dismissed. The fee of forgiveness requires me to treat the person who has hurt me as though they have never hurt me. Sometimes, if you want healing, you've got to be willing to demonstrate your forgiveness towards people who may have hurt you when they should've been helping you. You see, an indication that you are ready to live on new levels beyond the place of hurt is when you are willing and are actually following through with demonstrating forgiveness in the form of praying for

The Healing Experience

those who hurt you. Obviously, this fee of forgiveness is not an easy fee to cover. It can actually be one of the most expensive fees that we must pay and yet, if we want to be free from the levels of hurt that is oppressing us, we must be willing to pay the fee of forgiveness. And this fee is not something that you can simply pay outwardly, but the payment must actually begin inwardly. In other words, your heart must be invested in the payment process. One of the reasons why people seem stuck in the prison of their pain is because they haven't developed a heart that truly forgives. When your heart forgives, it will drive your head and your hands to forgive as well. When our heart forgives, declaration and demonstration will follow. You see, when our hearts are invested, forgiveness matures from being a moment to being a movement in our lives. When our heart is not in it, then we will struggle to maintain the payments that are needed to cover the fee for our freedom. You see, in order to be free from the oppression of our hurt, we must pay the fee of forgiveness and the challenge, is that the fee is not covered by a payment we make in a moment, but that fee constantly has interest in order to make sure that we never stop paying for it. The moment we stop paying the fee of forgiveness, that's when we will fall into the danger of being thrown back into the prison of oppression. The freedom that comes with the healing experience is one that requires a residual fee of forgiveness. The residual fee of forgiveness is a concept that is illustrated by Jesus in Matthew 18:21-22 (GNT). There it says, *21 Then Peter came to Jesus and asked, "Lord, if my brother keeps on sinning against me, how many times do I have to forgive him? Seven times?" 22 "No, not seven times," answered Jesus, "but seventy times seven..."* In other words, the fullness of the healing experience is going to require the repetition of release. The freedom that comes with the healing experience is going to require that we consistently and continuously operate with a heart of

The Healing Experience

forgiveness. When we mature to a place where our hearts have a nature of forgiveness, not only will we be able to pay the fee of forgiveness with repetition, but we will also be able to rebuke any restrictions placed on our need to release. Sometimes, when trying to live on new levels of life beyond the levels of hurt, we must be careful of the restrictions placed on our release or our forgiveness. Sometimes, there will be factors that will try to justify us putting restrictions on our forgiveness, but those restrictions will only compromise our restoration. The healing experience that we need requires us to finance it with the currency of forgiveness that is birthed out of your heart and transitions into your head and your hands. When we finally develop a heart to forgive people, both by what we communicate and what we demonstrate, then we will be able to experience life after the hurt that is twice as good as the life we had before we got hurt. This is what Job's healing experience reveals. Job's prayer was the expression of forgiveness that financed his healing experience that resulted in Job living on a level even greater than the level he was on, even prior to the hurt he experienced. This level of healing was made possible because Job developed a heart to forgive and that forgiveness was the currency needed to finance his healing experience from God. The more we can declare and demonstrate forgiveness from the heart, the more we will be able to shift from the levels of hurt to the levels of greater life. If we value the healing experience, then we must also value forgiveness. The reason forgiveness is so important to God, the reason why God would attach the manifestation of restoration to demonstration of forgiveness, is because that's the standard that God set; so much so that even Jesus, the Son of God, had to declare from the cross on which he was hanging, "Father forgive them, for they know not what they do." Jesus had the heart of the Father, he never allowed himself to be oppressed by the wounds of the cross. He

The Healing Experience

forgave and let the Father work it out in His favor. The demonstration of his forgiveness was seen in him dying for people who drove him to pain, yet, because he was willing to demonstrate forgiveness, the Father delivered him from pain and gave Jesus double for his trouble. Before the cross, Jesus was the son of God; but after the cross, he became the Son of God and the Savior of the world, who has all power in His hands. So, if we want to experience freedom to live beyond the hurt, we have to be determined to develop a heart that forgives. As you read this book, and particularly this section, let God stretch your heart towards a greater capacity of forgiveness. I want to challenge you in this area. Take some time to develop a list of people that require your demonstration of forgiveness. Pray and ask God to reveal names of people who have hurt you. After God gives you the list and you have written the names down, I want you to begin praying on how you can communicate and demonstrate authentic forgiveness towards them. After you pray about it, develop a plan of execution. Execute your demonstration of forgiveness.

Sometimes, you may discover that some people are seeking your forgiveness. Some of the names that God gives you may be people who aren't seeking forgiveness from you, nor do they feel they need it. As you release them repetitively, God will restore you and increase your life greater than you had before. If you find this to be too big of a challenge, don't feel bad at all. If you aren't at a place where you can forgive, if you're still struggling to demonstrate forgiveness, then be open to asking God to deal with you inwardly and directly. Begin to ask God if something exists internally that is allowing the memory of your wounds to oppress you beyond the lifespan of the wound itself. Begin to ask God to work on you and to operate on you. And for some of us, the reality is, forgiveness will require assistance. Forgiveness that is authentic may require you to get help on how to

The Healing Experience

reprogram your mind and your behavior so you can be consistent in repeating the release that is necessary to maintain your freedom. That assistance can be supernatural through intentional prayer and devotion time with God; it can be natural through counseling or high-level accountability partners. When going down the route of accountability partners, understand that accountability only works when accountability acquires authority. In other words, who are you authorizing to hold you accountable to the forgiveness that your freedom is requiring of you? Who are you authorizing to check you when your actions don't line up with the forgiveness that God holds you accountable to release, in order to experience the fullness of your healing experience? Again, the key is operating in forgiveness that fills our hearts and flows into our heads and our hands, in order to finance the freedom that comes with the fullness of God's healing experience for our lives.

The Healing Experience

The Healing Experience Notes:

CHAPTER FOUR

THERE IS DELIVERANCE IN DISCONNECTING

When seeking a healing experience from God, it is important to understand that God's agenda is never to simply Band-Aid the hurt with temporary impact or results. When God provides a healing experience, it is laced with longevity. It is given with the intentions of having lasting impact. The fruitfulness and fullness of the healing experience was meant to flourish with consistency in our lives. In order for the healing experience to maximize its full potential in our lives in a lasting way, healing requires the production of sustainable deliverance. When we speak of deliverance, we are simply speaking of freedom. We are speaking of liberation from any form of incarceration. What the healing experience seeks to do is establish a level of freedom, a level of lasting liberation from the imprisonment of our hurts. You see, the level of healing we experience is directly connected to the level of deliverance we experience. In order to have this sustained level of deliverance that results in sustained healing, the experience of deliverance will mandate that there be a moment of healing manifestation that then moves towards a movement of healing maintenance. In other words, if we want to be set free, our freedom will

The Healing Experience

need the partnership of our healing. If you are released from prison, but are not healed of the issues that resulted in your imprisonment, then your freedom will be short lived. What the healing experience does is, it seeks a moment in our freedom to usher in our healing. Now, in order for that healing to last, that freedom must last; but in order for the freedom to last, the healing must also last. What this means is healing needs maintenance, but so does deliverance. What we must deal with these in order to maximize the healing experience, to find a way to sustain our deliverance so that we can maintain our healing. If we are going to maintain our healing, which also requires that our deliverance is sustained, we must understand the power of disconnection. True deliverance requires disconnection. If the healing experience is going to manifest and be maintained in our lives, it will require the maintenance work of severance from the sources of our suffering. The maintenance that makes the healing experience fully effective in our lives is done through our decisions to disconnect or sever from anything that is causing consistent damage in our lives. There are people, some places and some opportunities that have the potential and the power to disrupt our deliverance, thus delaying our healing. Sometimes the only way to ensure that the healing experience is manifested and maintained is to learn to disconnect ourselves from those connections. Whatever is causing our hurts to transition beyond the temporary status that it should have, if we are going to experience healing from it so we can move forward without it, then we must understand that we can't afford to continue to live with it, but we've got to get loosed from it, even if it means we must make the decision to end it, so that we're not being held hostage to it.

In pursuing the healing experience, here is a powerful question that the healing experience is going to require us to wrestle with: Are you willing to unplug in order to get unstuck? Let's expand the

The Healing Experience

framework of that question by asking it this way: Are you willing to disconnect in order to maintain the authority of your deliverance, which then makes the healing experience effective and enduring in your life? As we go through the process towards healing, we must be willing to make decisions that demonstrate how much we value healing and it's sustainability in our lives. To determine this, we will have to gage our determination by our willingness to make difficult decisions to disconnect from anything that may be hindering us from healing. Consider the hurts that you have experienced or may still be experiencing in your life and ask yourself the following: *What is it in my life that is causing this hurt to maintain its residency in my life? Who or what is it that I remain connected to that continues to be an open door for hurt to occupy my space? Where is it that every time I go there, the hurt seems to find enough life and strength that allows it to refuse to leave me alone?* If we honestly take time to wrestle with these questions, we may discover that there may be connections in our lives that are compromising the conclusions that the healing experience is intended to customize for our lives. During pastoral counseling opportunities, I have seen this concept play out time and time again. People will remain in relationships that provide maintenance to the damage and dysfunction that they have experienced rather than disconnect from the relationship and take advantage of the opportunity to heal their lives. I remember counseling a couple who had determined that they were going to get married. During the counseling session, I was able to discern that while this couple possessed genuine love for one another, they were not ready to experience the totality of the journey of marriage. Both had experienced hurt at the hands of the other and neither had taken the time to heal from the hurts that were experienced. They had not done anything to deeply address and deal with the hurts that they caused one another. As we reached the end of

The Healing Experience

the numerous sessions, I informed them that my conclusion is that I could not sign off on their marriage because they were not ready. Later on, they eventually unplugged from the relationship. After a year or so, I saw the woman and I asked her about their relationship. She informed me that they had broken up and that she realized the truth that she didn't want to acknowledge, that truth was they were not healthy together. She went on to tell me that while they tried their best to work on the relationship, she realized that there was too much hurt experienced and she would not be able to get her life together while continuing to be in a relationship with him. Recently, my wife and I were at a wedding and we ran into one of our friends whom we have not seen in a long time. She informed us that she was no longer married and how it was the best decision for her life. She told us that during the marriage, even when it was clear that the marriage was beyond repair and that it was ruining her life, she continued to stay connected because she loved her husband, she wanted to honor her wedding vows and not disappoint God. As a result, she remained stuck in a marriage that consistently manifested mayhem and misery. As much as she tried to do the work, it only resulted in her further damage. After years of trying to honor and bring healing to her marriage, she finally made the difficult decision to disconnect from her marriage. It wasn't until she made the decision to disconnect that she was able to even begin the process of healing. You see, sometimes, we struggle to heal because we're still holding on to hope that something is going to happen that will fix everything in our favor. We maintain hope that one day, the other person will participate in the process; we maintain hope that one day, God will miraculously do the work for us that will result in our healing; and then, for some of us, we struggle to heal because we remain connected to relationships due to our theology disapproving of certain disconnections, particularly in the case of marriage. We begin to

The Healing Experience

take scriptures and apply them to our situations, hoping that the scriptures and even our efforts to apply them and do practical work will troubleshoot the issues that are troubling our connections. The challenge however, is sometimes, when it comes to certain connections, whether it be our connection to people, places or even opportunities, God will sometimes determine that disconnection is necessary. While we may do our best to work and pray and believe God to bring about transformation to our connections, God may have already determined that we must experience termination from those connections. Regardless of how much we pray and fast and request God to fix it, we have to understand that God won't work towards transformation, when He has determined the connection needs termination. When it comes to healing, there are some connections you can't work through, but you have to walk away from. Because we are believing God for healing that is continuous and lasting; healing that will manifest and be maintained, we have to be ready for the work of disconnection. Again, the process gets more challenging the deeper we dive into it. You see, our hurts will always have a warrant for our arrest until we put a halt to what we allow to be attached. Here's what we have to remember; the wrong attachments become warrants for our arrest. God loves us. His love is determined and driven to see us healed and whole. God will sometimes create experiences within the healing experience process, where healing will require God to intervene and cause what is hurting, cause what is draining life from us, cause what is standing in the way of us making progress and prospering in our lives beyond the places of our pain, and our disappointments and our hurts, God will cause those connections to be cancelled so that they don't undermine the healing conclusion that He intends for us to live in. If you take some time to honestly assess your life, you may discover that there were some connections that you may have had to some people,

The Healing Experience

some things, some places, and some opportunities in your life that ended up dying or coming to an end. When it happened, you weren't expecting it to happen, you didn't want it to happen, you probably even prayed against it happening, but it still came to an end.

Sometimes, the reason experiences like this happen is because, while we may want certain connections to continue in our lives, God determines and decides that in order to move us forward from it, in order for us to get past the hurt and disappointment and the lack of progress that some connections may be causing in our lives, God must create or allow conditions that will cause it to die out of our lives. If you really think about it, you can probably think of some relationships or some opportunities that you thought you needed or some places that you thought you couldn't stay away from that just shut down in your life; it just broke down; it became close to you without any reasons as to why it happened. Could it be that God allowed it to die or caused it to die in order to ensure your deliverance and the sustainability of your healing? When you begin to further understand the heart of God the Father, then you will understand that before God, your heavenly Father, lets the connection hurt you again, before God allows it to keep you from doing what He called you to do. Before God allows it to impact your life any longer, the decision would have already been made to bring to an end, what is having a negative impact on your progress, on you being healthy beyond the hurt that was caused by that particular connection. In other words, the decision that God will sometimes make is this: Some things need to die so you can get and stay delivered. For some of us, this may be a present reality. We may find ourselves dealing with connections today that may actually need to die or come to an end and we must be willing to either execute that decision or embrace God's execution of that decision in our lives. At the end of the day, here's what an authentic healing experience may really boil down

The Healing Experience

to; your healing experience may demand the partnership between deliverance and disconnection.

I want to present this biblical story to demonstrate the power of disconnecting, and how important it is to our healing. In the gospel of Matthew 21:18-19 NRSV, we find a very brief story that may not seem to be significant, but it possesses great power in the principles that it teaches, and these principles are critical for healing. The scripture reads like this: *18 In the morning, when he returned to the city, he was hungry. 19 And seeing a fig tree by the side of the road, he went to it and found nothing at all on it but leaves. Then he said to it, "May no fruit ever come from you again!" And the fig tree withered at once.* Here is Jesus traveling back with his disciples into the city and on their way, they stop at a fig tree to get something to eat. When they get to the tree, they are left disappointed because the tree failed to provide what they needed. The tree didn't have any fruit for them to eat. They were trying to connect to a tree that could not provide their need. I need you to see this. This tree was planted, purposed and positioned to produce something to help them deal with the issue of their hunger. This tree was supposed to help them overcome the experience of being hungry, but in the connection that they make with this tree, they discover that their connection with this tree is only perpetuating their state of hunger. The tree is causing their hunger to linger.

And while this is a minor experience of disappointment, which can open the door for hurt, many people who need healing today are dealing with hurt and disappointment because of the failures of who or what they are connecting to in life. Many people are connecting to trees that should be helping them heal from their experience of being hungry, but the trees are only leaving them imprisoned in the same state of hunger. As much as we may try to get past some hurts in our lives, as much as we try to overcome it, hurtful experiences will continue to negatively impact us; hurtful experiences will continue to have a hold on us if we don't partner our deliverance with disconnection. While we may do all we can to get past the hurt, sometimes the only way to really be healed of the hurt is to cut off any source that is sustaining the status of our suffering. For the rest of this section, we are going to talk about warning signs, indicators, red flags to look for; breaking points to establish as a determining factor of whether a disconnection needs to take place in order to sustain the level of deliverance that makes healing last in our lives. In other words, at what point must we declare that a disconnection is needed in order for healing to both manifest and be maintained?

A. Feeding without Flourishing

So let's look at the scripture again. The bible says, *18 In the morning, when he returned to the city, he was hungry. 19 And seeing a fig tree by the side of the road, he went to it and found nothing at all on it but leaves. Then he said to it, "May no fruit ever come from you again!" And the fig tree withered at once.* Jesus and the disciples are on a journey back to the city; they stop for food at a place that should be able to feed them, but it fails to do so. Sometimes, we connect and establish relationships with people and with opportunities that should be able to feed us, but the results are that we who should be fed seem to be left in a famished condition. This presents a tremendous challenge to our healing. You see, we will always struggle to heal if we are internally famished and fatigued even after feeding off of the connection. This is a warning sign that should not be ignored. This is an indicator that it may be time for disconnection. If your connection or

The Healing Experience

your relationship or your dealings with someone leaves you famished or fatigued, if it leaves you still feeling empty and exhausted, then that is a connection that you may not be able to afford while you are trying to heal. One of the most dangerous and destructive things we can do to our healing process is stay connected to the wrong people and things and places, particularly if those connections do more to drain us than they deposit into our lives. We have to be very careful of our connections, especially when we are going through a healing process, because our connections can help provide us with necessities for our healing. The right connections can provide needed encouragement and support. The right connection can feed us measures of motivation and inspiration that will be necessary during the process towards healing. God will use connections to help us experience the manifestation and maintenance of healing. Conversely, feeding off of the wrong connections can certainly hinder our experience of healing. Feeding off of the wrong connections can open the door to discouragement and discontentment. If we feed off of connections that are not providing the nutrients that are conducive to our healing, if we feed off of connections that are leaving us discouraged and feeling discontent, it puts our healing in great danger. The danger of feeding off of these connections that leave us discouraged and feeling discontent is that these feelings become doors of opportunity that the devil can use to help delay the manifestation or disrupt the maintenance of healing in our lives. Here is a demonic strategy to stifle and suppress our healing experience. The devil will use these open doors of discouragement and discontentment to further invite associative demonic elements such as the spirit of depression, despair, despondency and defeat. When these doors become open in our lives, particularly during a healing process, it makes healing that much more difficult to be experienced. When you are trying to experience healing or trying to cause healing to endure in

The Healing Experience

your life, the connections in our lives become critical to our experiences. Sometimes, we remain stuck in places of hurt because we maintain connections that should be able to add something to us that's going to make us stronger; they should add something that is going to help us recover from the experiences that have hurt us or disappointed us and left us in a state of being imprisoned by the experience; they should make us more ready and durable for the journey of life that we're on, but instead, they end up leaving us disappointed and unfulfilled. Here's a very critical principle to the healing experience. The healing experience will seek to disconnect you when the deposits are not driving you towards greater development. When we are trying to heal or maintain our healing, we must be careful of connections that consistently fail to properly feed us because the body can't flourish if it's not being fed. Healing can't flourish in your life if you are connecting to people, things and places that are not pouring the right things in you. You can't properly grow and make positive progress if your connections fail to feed you the nutrients you need to heal and move past your hurts. In working with people, I have learned that many people can make progress even without the process of healing their hurts, but with their progress often comes pollution. While they can experience great success, it is often saturated with the stain of suffering that they never had the suitable support system to help them address and overcome. When we are able to feed off of our connections to the right people, places and the pursuit of the right opportunities, the probability of experiencing God's healing in our lives increases tremendously. Now, because the feeding process is so critical to the healing experience, God will sometimes cause the healing process to become challenging to us by cutting connections or creating conditions that will cut connections that do more to feed off of us, than they do to feed us. So here's the principle: *When healing, you may have to flee*

The Healing Experience

from connections that do more to fleece you than feed you. Sometimes, we struggle to experience and maintain healing in our lives because we are holding on to connections that aren't adding anything to us, but seem to always take something away from us. While you are trying to experience healing and when trying to maintain healing, be careful of getting fleeced when you are needing to feed. In this season, it becomes important that we pray for a level of discernment that will help us identify if our connections are conning us. We have to pray that God would enlighten the eyes of our understanding so that we may know if the connections that look like and may even act like they are helping us, really have nothing of value to add to our lives when we really get to know who they are at the core. The fig tree was dysfunctional because it looked like it should have been able to provide some food, but all it had was leaves. It should've been able to feed Jesus real substance to help Him flourish in His physical strength but it failed to do so. It should've been able to add something of value in Jesus and his disciples, but it failed to do so. Some of us are struggling to heal and move forward because we remain attached and connected to dysfunctional people, dysfunctional groups, dysfunctional jobs and dysfunctional churches, that are not depositing anything of value in us, but rather, are leaving us in a state of dysfunction that keeps us victimized by the hurts we have experienced in our lives.

This would have been the contributions of that particular fig tree, if Jesus would have maintained that connection. Jesus would have continued in a connection that can't feed him what he needs to overcome his issue of hunger. This presents a situation for Jesus. He has connected with this particular tree in order to help him conquer his condition of hunger, but the tree is only able to provide leaves. If we contemporize the situation, here are a few options that Jesus had. Jesus could have simply settled for what the tree was able to offer him. Jesus

The Healing Experience

could have taken his power and transformed the leaves into something that was more suitable for his taste. When we think about this from the perspective of connections we have with people, places and opportunities, many people end up settling with whatever our connections are able to offer us even if it's not healthy for us. Using the second option, many people will do their best to make it work. Even though the connections are failing them, they will use their resources to try to make the best out of a bad connection. Now, let's go over the option that Jesus chose. When Jesus sees the tree and its inability to properly feed him, Jesus neither settles for the leaves nor does Jesus use his resources to make the tree produce something that Jesus would like, but rather Jesus simply destroys his connection to the tree. He cuts the connection by cursing the tree. The moment He curses the tree, that tree would no longer be able to provide any substance, which then removes the purpose of connecting to that tree. What this teaches us about healing is this: When trying to heal, don't allow desperation to delay or deny the decision of disconnection that is needed to maintain your deliverance. If you are in a connection just because it makes you feel better, but it's not helping you be better, then it may be a warning sign that you may want to disconnect. If you feel better, but your behavior is not better; if you feel better, but your life is still toxic; your attitude is still terrible; bitterness is still rising out of you, then that relationship is not empowering you to heal, it's enabling you to remain hurt and you can't allow yourself to be dependent on those kind of connections, especially when you are healing. The power of the healing experience is that it will disconnect connections where our dependency helps to sustain the dysfunctional dominance of our hurt. It becomes so critical to pay attention to our connections because they are critical to both the manifestation and the maintenance of our healing experience. They allow a level of deliverance that makes

The Healing Experience

healing last. As you move forward towards healing, begin to assess the connections in your life. Pray and ask God for the grace to cut connections that are keeping you in captivity to your hurt. I believe God will provide the grace you need to make those difficult decisions of disconnection. If, however, we struggle to make those difficult decisions, we can rest assured that the love of God will intervene on behalf of the healing that He desires for our lives. Sometimes, because we can get too comfortable and too connected to end connections ourselves, God will have to step in and create conditions or allow circumstances to happen in order to bring some connections to an end. This may be the explanation when we begin to see connections breaking off of our lives. When we start to clash with people beyond repair or when people start to walk out of our lives or we experience betrayals, while they may hurt us initially, we must pray and seek God to see if God is communicating the need for those connections to come to an end. Sometimes, God will let you know that these experiences we are having in our connections are divinely orchestrated and are being done in such a way that they will never be able to produce anything that will be worth your connection to it again. As you move forward towards greater healing experiences in your life, don't disregard the warning signs within connections that feed you, but the feeding doesn't help you flourish towards living your best life beyond the hurts that you have experienced.

B. Potential without Production

Another important warning sign or red flag that helps indicate the need to disconnect in order to manifest or maintain healing in our lives is having potential without production. Let's go back to the connection

The Healing Experience

that Jesus makes with this fig tree in Matthew 21, particularly verse 19. There, the scripture records: *19 And seeing a fig tree by the side of the road, he went to it and found nothing at all on it but leaves.* In this part of the story, Jesus sees the fig tree. He identifies what kind of tree it is, and based on what He sees, Jesus understood that there should be a particular product that this particular tree was given the potential to produce. You see, the leaves on the tree helped identify the kind of tree that He saw. The leaves became an indication to Jesus that there should have been some kind of production of fruit based on the potential that he saw in the leaves of that particular tree. Jesus understood that fig trees always have the potential to produce fruit whenever their leaves were present, yet, when he approaches this particular fig tree that had leaves, he didn't see the production of fruit based on the potential that the tree had, due to the leaves that were hanging on the tree. In our connections, we have to be careful, that we can identify both potential and production. Sometimes, we perpetuate our state of hurt and disappointment because we stay connected to people because we believe the connection has the potential to help us become better, only to discover that the potential never evolves beyond the state of potential. When healing is the conclusion we are after, we have to be careful of connections that have great potential, but never progresses towards great production. When the connection continues to fail to produce what you need to help you make progress in your life beyond the hurts you have experienced, then that may be a warning sign that it may not be the right connection for you. During the process towards healing, we can't afford to maintain connections that keep failing to produce according to its potential. While God plants potential in us, God expects production from us. *God doesn't plant any seed that He doesn't expect to grow into a harvest.* Every person that God puts in our lives is a seed that He planted with the expectation of bringing

The Healing Experience

some form of increase into our lives. The right connections are planted as potential that eventually progresses into a point of production. No one whom God connects you to should simply remain in a state of potentiality. Their presence in your life should present and provide a level of production that can help you make progress towards living a life that reflects God's healing in your life. They should produce something that can satisfy the potential that God placed in them when He planted them in your life. If we are serious about our healing, we must become serious about connecting with people who have the potential to actually produce substance that will help you. Think about your connections. Think about your opportunities or your friendships and assess whether the connections are able and are actually depositing or providing something that can help you heal. This work of assessing our connections is so important to our healing because many people have connections and some of those connections are dear to their heart, but the problem is, these connections are standing on a foundation of potential, but they keep failing to produce anything that helps those who have been hurt and are being held hostage to their hurts, transition to a state of experiencing the kind of life that only God's healing can provide. Potential alone has no real substance. The wrong connections will demonstrate the potential to help you heal, but will struggle to develop real substance to help you progress from your hurt. Healing will not manifest and be maintained if you only operate on connections that have the potential to help, but aren't producing helpful substance in your life. This was the problem with the fig tree to which Jesus connected. As long as that tree could not produce according to the potential it possessed, the issue of hunger would continue. Hence, Jesus determined that He was better off without it. If healing is our desire and determination, we can't allow ourselves to be made prisoners of potential because potential will always have us in a position of

The Healing Experience

anticipation, without ever advancing towards actualization. For example, if your counselor has the potential to help you heal, but every time you leave that counselor, you feel more discouraged and more dysfunctional, then you may need to assess if that counselor is effective enough to help you with your concerns. You can continue to go to the sessions hoping that something will be different after the next session; you can continue to have a positive attitude and believe that the counselor is going to do something to help you break through, but at some point, you are going to have to come to the realization that the counselor, while they may have the potential, their potential is powerless to help you if it can't produce accordingly. If we are seriously pursuing an authentic healing experience, at some point, we may have to disconnect from connections that have potential but can never seem to produce accordingly.

C. Presentation without Proof

The last important warning sign or red flag that I want to highlight that helps indicate the need to disconnect in order to manifest or maintain healing in our lives, is when a connection has presentation without proof. This principle is also found in the connection that Jesus makes with the fig tree. Let's look at verse 19 again: *19 And seeing a fig tree by the side of the road, he went to it and found nothing at all on it but leaves.* When Jesus sees this tree, He pursues it because of the presentation that suggested that the tree would have fruit. Sometimes we pursue and go after various connections because the presentation satisfied our preferences. While presentation is important, if there is no proof of what is being presented, then we must be careful of that

The Healing Experience

particular partnership. There are people who struggle to heal because they were drawn by the presentation, but never checked for the proof. The presentation was a pretense. Like the fig tree, the presentation has leaves and we get so excited about the leaves that we forget to check for the fruit.

Sometimes, our relationships and our connections are beautiful presentations on the surface, but they have no proof beneath the surface. They intentionally put on a show to get you attached, only to later discover that it was all false advertisement. As a result, when healing, we must be careful of connecting to people that present healing as their reality without proof that they are actually living healed in their reality. These kind of connections will only produce deceptive results because they are rooted in deception. This is a satanic strategy that we must be aware of; the enemy will try to strategically put people in our lives who will possess great presentation just to establish partnership with us, but by the time we discover that what they presented was nothing more than a pretense, a hoax, a façade we would have already been hurt and damaged by the connection. How many people do you know who pursued and parked in a relationship because they thought the other person really loved them, but later, they discovered that the person they pursued and partnered with may have only been pretending to love them in order to establish a connection with them for their own personal gain. When a connection has great presentation, but is void of proof of what was presented, then that is a warning sign that must not be taken lightly. As a result, during our healing process, it becomes critical that we allow discernment to help identify necessary disconnections. If we're not careful, we can get mesmerized by presentations. We can get caught up in what people seem to be and what they can seem to do, but careless in who they are based on what they have already done or are still doing. While they appear to be able

The Healing Experience

to help better our lives, the reality is, there is nothing about their lives that prove that they will be able to help us heal or become better in our lives. This was another problem with the fig tree. The fig tree had the right presentation, but it had no proof. It had the potential, but it had no proof that the potential would actually lead to production. This is where we have to connect with caution. You have to assess the proof. You have to check the credentials of the one to whom you are connected. Assess whether or not they have the credentials to help. If they are going to help you heal, is there evidence that they are healed themselves? Do they demonstrate behavior that communicates they are living in God's freedom or does their behavior demonstrate that there is unaddressed brokenness and bondage in their own lives? If there are concerns about the credentials or the proof of their capacity to help you heal, don't ignore them. Don't disregard the lack of proof or credential just because the presentation fits our hopeful destination. When healing is the conclusion we are after, we have to be careful not to allow costumes to create cover-ups for necessary credentials. An authentic healing experience is going to require connections with authentic people who aren't simply putting on a front or a facade just to get your attention. The healing experience we need will require connections with people who aren't simply putting on a show just to draw us into their circles. When we discover the lack of proof or the lack of credentials that may be a warning sign or a red flag to disconnect. What we must consider is that, what is presented as an opportunity for healing, may actually be opposition to our healing outcome. Jesus immediately ended his connection to this fig tree that presented leaves that had no fruit. Even if it wasn't the fig tree's season to produce fruit, because it had leaves, it should've produced fruit, even if the fruit would not have been ripened. Regardless of the connection, pay attention to the proof beneath the presentation. If they are presenting

The Healing Experience

that they are healed, but can't demonstrate proof of their healing, then consider disconnecting. If they are presenting that they have love in their hearts, but can't demonstrate that love, then that lack of proof can't be ignored. Take seriously the warning signs that may be communicating the need to make a decision towards disconnection. The disconnection may not be permanent, but it may have to be prioritized in order to manifest or maintain healing in one's life.

The Healing Experience

The Healing Experience Notes:

CHAPTER FIVE

LIVING THE HEALED LIFE

This book was systematically and strategically written to empower individuals with spiritual, yet practical tools that can help position people for the manifestation of healing experiences in life. I believe by reaching this point of the book, you have already made a level of progress towards the fullness of your healing experience and that alone, is worth celebrating. Before we go on any further, please take some time to celebrate your progress. If for no other reason, celebrate the commitment and consistency that you have been able to exercise by simply in taking and prayerfully, internalizing the information and insight within this book. You see, this process towards healing and the process towards reaching any place of prosperity (success) can be very discouraging and draining, which can then prolong or even prevent us from fully experiencing the prize that we were pursuing. Sometimes, what provides us with the power we need to endure the process is learning to embrace the progress.

Regardless of how small or insignificant the progress may seem, learn to acknowledge it and celebrate it while you are still pursuing the ultimate prize. Dr. Martin Luther King once stated, *"Human progress is neither automatic nor inevitable... Every step toward the goal of justice*

The Healing Experience

requires sacrifice, suffering, and struggle; the tireless exertions and passionate concern of dedicated individuals." Again, this level of progress must not be taken lightly. Getting to this point is a big deal. While we must be careful not to dwell in progress, we must also be careful that we don't disregard our progress as well. The reason it is so important to celebrate this is because the level of progress that you have made towards your healing experience is not something that could be reached accidentally or coincidentally; rather, it required you to make sacrifices, even if that sacrifice was simply the time you took to read the information. To experience the full extent of the progress this book is intended to provide for you, it will require your tireless exertions and passionate concerns. The fullness of the healing experience will require a level of sacrifice; it will require you to struggle with the various details of your past and present that may be contributing to your hurting state. It is not an experience that we get to automatically or inevitably receive simply because we are alive or because we are the children of God. While we have access to God's healing experiences, while it is available to us, it is up to us to do the work that this book and other resources may provide to assist us in experiencing the progress that the healing experience can produce and provide in our lives.

Up to this point, the attempt has been to lay out practical principles to assist in providing a healing experience. I believe that while it is important to experience healing in our lives, it is just as important to live in the healing that has been experienced. As discussed earlier in this book, healing should not simply end at the moment of manifestation, but it should mature into a movement of maintenance in our lives. This movement of maintenance is at the heart of living a healed life. The impact of the healing experience is not simply the experience of healing, but it is also the extension of healing and that extension requires maintenance. In other words, when we experience

The Healing Experience

healing from God, it is not simply given to get us healed, but it is given so that we can live healed. Regardless of the hurt, it is possible to live healed. It is possible to maintain the manifestation of healing in our lives. Oftentimes, when we are trying to experience healing, the results seem to leave us in a rollercoaster state of existence where we are healed today, but then hurt comes back to take control tomorrow. Healing seems to be a constant up and down, back and forth experience. It comes without consistency; it shows up, yet lacks stability. Yet, the fullness of God's healing experience comes with power to push us past the hurt and power to persist in our healing long after the initial healing moment took place in our lives.

I want to establish the proper understanding of the healed life so that we aren't confused about our experiences beyond this moment. When we talk about the healed life and living the healed life, what does that mean and what does that look like from a practical standpoint? To be clear, living the healed life doesn't mean living life without hurt. Being healed doesn't mean you are free from hurt. It doesn't mean you won't experience struggles and moments of pain in your life. You will still experience hits that will hurt; you will continue to experience problems and trials and tribulations; these experiences come with the territory of being human. This is important to understand because if we're not careful, we can negate and nullify the work of healing with our mouths because the facts of what may be hitting our lives may not line up with the fruit of healing that God has already established in our lives. I want to make sure that we clearly understand what the healed life is not. It is not a life free of hurt. Such a life does not exist in our humanity. The idea of living healed is birthed from the understanding of the revelation that Jesus provides in the gospel of John 16:33 when He said, *"In this life, you will have tribulation; but be of good cheer for I have already overcome the world."* In the context of healing, what

The Healing Experience

that means is that even though we may experience hurt, because of Christ, the hurt can't hold us hostage.

When you are living the healed life, hurt loses the authority to hold you hostage. At the heart of the healed life is this understanding: while we can be healed and still experience hurt, we can't be healed and surrender to a hostage situation. The evidence of the healed life is found in the power to experience the hurt without letting the hurt dominate your decisions. One of the greatest indicators of someone who is not living the healed life is when their decisions are made or not made because of the hurt they have experienced in life. They make a decision to stay single because of a relationship that hurt them; they make a decision to stay on the job because they were hindered by the experience of trying to start a business, only to discover that no one would buy their product. As a result, they refuse to try again, even though the opportunities keep knocking at their door. When you are struggling to take forward steps without the influence of your hurts, it is a sign that healing has not matured in your life. While you may have experienced a moment of healing, your moment never matured into a movement where it is being maintained to the degree that you are free from the imprisonment of that experience. When living the healed life, hurt should no longer be able to use fear to faze or freeze you from authentically being the best version of yourself. Think about your decisions in life; think about potential decisions in your future that require your attention and address the following questions: *Am I making choices and behaving in ways due to the fear that I may get hurt again? Am I about to make choices and behave in ways that are primarily due to the fear of what may happen if it fails again? Am I strategizing according to the struggles and sufferings of past seasons? Are my plans simply the product of being puppeteered by my pain?* Somewhere along the way, the hurt that was experienced from

The Healing Experience

betrayals and from rejection or from failure may not have been healed or at best, only experienced healing that has yet to mature. Somewhere along the way, the hurt you experienced from that relationship or that business not working or being rejected by that job or being abandoned by your parents or being violated by some authority figure in your life has not experienced the maturity of God's healing experience. It is very possible that the hurt that you thought was healed, may not have been healed. It may be healing, but it's not healed. When it gets healed, the maturation of healing, the fullness of the healing experience empowers you to make decisions and to live your life independent of and in spite of the hurt that you have experienced in the past or may be experiencing in your present. This is the power and purpose of the healing experience. God wants us to experience healing that shifts us from hurt to a level of healing that can be maintained beyond the moment of its manifestation. This is the maturation of the healing experience that I believe God is providing for you today. At the heart of the healing experience are tools to help us live the healed life. These principles I believe are pinpointed and revealed in the prophetic writing of the Old Testament prophet, Isaiah. Let's consider and contemplate the Word of the Lord given to the prophet to prophesy to people of God:

> *18 But the Lord says, "Do not cling to events of the past or dwell on what happened long ago. 19 Watch for the new thing I am going to do. It is happening already - you can see it now! I will make a road through the wilderness and give you streams of water there. 20 Even the wild animals will honor me; jackals and ostriches will praise me when I make rivers flow in the desert to give water to my*

The Healing Experience

chosen people. 21 They are the people I made for myself, and they will sing my praises!" (Isaiah 43:18-21 GNT)

This is a powerful prophetic word that can be contextualized without compromising the integrity of the text. This word is given to the people of Israel as a word of healing and restoration. They found themselves seemingly stuck in a rut because they wanted their facts to line up with the former life they knew. They were remembering and reminiscing about what God had done historically, and as a result, they became restrained from receiving what God was about to do in their current reality. They were hurt as a people and so God sends this prophetic word of healing and restoration. In this prophetic word, the prophet includes verses 18-21, where God provides strategies to support their healing so that it is sustained long after the word is supplied. I believe as we utilize these strategies properly, we can tap into the maturity of our healing that makes it possible to live the healed life.

A. Combat the Compulsion to Cling

One of the challenges to experiencing healing in our lives is the tendency to cling. If we aren't careful with the hurts of life, the experience can create a compulsion in us to cling to the core of that hurt. Hurt can develop a desire to dwell in domains that displaces us from our deliverance. I want to make sure I am placing enough emphasis on this principle being one of the biggest hindrances to living a healed life. Nothing hinders healing more than trying to dwell in places that God delivered us from. Often, this dwelling or this clinging

The Healing Experience

to our past begins as a simple memory. We've talked about this previously, but I want to deal with it at a deeper level. Before we stated that what keeps us stuck in our state of hurt is the memory that becomes a monument and monuments are meant to be stared at; they are intended to grab and grip our attention. They are big enough to influence our entire view. As a result, when our hurts are not properly dealt with, hurts become monuments that we continue to stare at and become fixated on. While the memory becoming a monument in our lives is troubling and dangerous to our healing, consider this as an even greater danger to the healing experience: *Memories that become monuments will mesmerize us until it masters us. In other words, the memory of that hurt eventually becomes the master of our movements in life.* That's warfare that we must consider; the devil wants to become the master of our movements by causing us to become mesmerized by our memories. All of a sudden, the memory that was a point of reference turns into a place of residence; and if we stay in that place of residence too long, it will regulate our lives. To disrupt and dismantle the impact of clinging, God provides this strategic principle to *not cling to the events of the past or dwell on what happened long ago*. Let's consider what God is not saying so that we can have clarity on what God is saying. God is not saying that we should negate our past or even disregard our past. Many people struggle to heal because they negate or disregard what they have been through. They don't even deal with it. They simply sweep it under the rug of concealment and simply try to move on with life. They even consider it a demonstration or expression of their faith. This perspective is distorted at best. Faith never requires you to negate the facts, but rather acknowledge what has happened to further give evidence of God's power to overcome the facts that may be standing in the way of the desired conclusion. Remember, in order for healing to be experienced, hurt must be in existence. If you are

The Healing Experience

hurting, please understand that God's strategy of not clinging is not a call to negate or disregard what you have been through or what you are going through. When God instructs the people not to cling, God is identifying our internal capacity to dwell on our past. God is telling the people not to dwell on what they have been through. In other words, when you are trying to heal and move forward in your healing, be careful not to get mesmerized by the memory of what you've been through. Regardless of how often the memory infiltrates the space in your mind, don't allow your mind to become rental space for that memory. Don't hold on to it and here is why holding on is so dangerous to the healing experience. You see, whatever you hold on to, you will hold up for. In other words, if you hold on to the past, you will hold up everything in your life for the past. Everything will be put on pause because you are still holding on to something that has happened at the expense of everything that is and could be happening in your life. Notice that God says *"Don't cling;"* this is given in the imperative form. In basic grammar, we learn that the imperative is not a suggestion, but it's a command. Now, God only gives commands when God knows there is the capacity to meet that command; now granted, the capacity will often require his collaboration and contribution, but nonetheless, it's a command. So that when God says, don't cling, it's because God knows that with His help, it can be done. If you find yourself struggling to move beyond the memory of your hurt or you can't seem to get it out of your thought life, understand that regardless of how damaging the experience was, with God's help, you have the capacity to comply with this command to not cling. Now, let's continue with the grammatical presentation of the imperative form of this strategy to not cling. In basic English grammar, we learned that in addition to the imperative being a command, it also has an unidentified subject, who is always the person receiving the command. What this

The Healing Experience

means is when God says don't cling, the question is, who is the subject or who is God commanding not to cling; and the answer is, whoever is hearing or receiving the command. If you are hearing or receiving the command, then that command would imply, *You,* don't cling. Now scripturally, He's speaking to Israel, but in terms of revelation, He's speaking to whoever is listening. For the sake of review, the command to not cling is given because God knows with His help, we will have the capacity to comply with the command that He is giving. This understanding leads to a deeper revelation within this strategic principle. If we are going to combat the compulsion to cling so we can live the healed life, we must own our capacity to control the conduct of our consciousness. With God's collaboration and contribution to help us comply with this command to not cling, there is a level of authority that we acquire in God that we are now accountable to use in order to control any conduct that flows from our consciousness. In other words, whatever thought invades your mind, because of God's help, you have the authority to control how it manifests in your behavior. You see, the healed life mandates that we learn to become masters of our mind. While we can't always control the content of our mind, we can control the conduct that flows from our mind. And so, if we are serious about living healed, we have to become serious about mastering our mind because whoever or whatever becomes the master of your mind, will master your movements in life. It becomes the responsibility of the child of God to control the conduct that is cultivated from his or her consciousness. Ultimately, to combat the compulsion to cling to your past and to your hurts, you can't let the memory master you, but you must become master of the memory. Because of God's help, you get to choose what you do with the thoughts that you think. Here are some principles to help you master your mind so you can combat the compulsion to cling. First, you must **imprison** the Memory before it

The Healing Experience

infects your Mind. In 2 Corinthians 10:5, The Apostle Paul says, *Take Captive every thought to make it obedient to Christ.*

In other words, when a memory shows up, a war has been declared and you have to act quickly and decisively on who is going to be in control, you or that memory. You must take it captive before it makes you its captive. You have to quickly subdue it; bring it under subjection; capture it quickly. Don't give it the freedom to roam in your mind. As soon as it manifests, as soon as the thought infiltrates your mind, acknowledge it, arrest it and then evict it out of your mind. If you give too much space to the memory, it will spoil the mind. If you entertain it, you further establish its existence in your life. The second principle to mastering our mind is to replace what we have removed.

In Isaiah 26:3, the bible says, *for thou shall keep in peace, those whose mind are stayed on you*; and In Philippians 4:8, the Apostle Paul says this: *"Finally, brothers and sisters, whatever is true, whatever is noble, whatever is right, whatever is pure, whatever is lovely, whatever is admirable--if anything is excellent or praiseworthy--think about such things."* When you are trying to master your mind so you can combat the compulsion to cling, it isn't enough to simply arrest and evict the thoughts or memories in our mind; it isn't enough to just remove them, but after we remove them, something else must replace what was in that space. As you try to combat the compulsion to cling, take some time to assess what thoughts are you allowing to fill your mind; what material are you moving into the space of your mind. The mind will be filled whether you fill it or not. You have to fill your mind because if you don't fill your mind, the devil will fill it for you. This is part of the devil's warfare strategy against us. The devil is trying to fill our mind with negative thoughts because the devil can fill our mind, then the devil can force our movements in life. The warfare is a constant battle back and forth for space in our mind. To win the battle, the devil will try to bombard you with thoughts and memories that can reprogram your mind to be subject to the negativity of those memories and thoughts. On the other hand, God's strategy calls for you to bombard your mind with thoughts that are subjected to the Holy Spirit and the Word of God instead of being imprisoned to our memories. To assist in this warfare, God supplies us with support systems in the form of the scriptures, worship gatherings, Godly relationships and professional counseling. Resources like these can help us fill our mind with thoughts that can help counter the demonic attempt to mesmerize the mind until the memory becomes the master of the mind. This is the idea behind the words of the Apostle Paul to the Philippian church when he says this in Philippians 4:8 *In conclusion, my friends, fill your minds with those things that are good and that deserve praise: things that are true, noble, right, pure, lovely, and honorable. (Philippians 4:8 GNT)* The more you can fill your mind with thoughts that represent God and His will for your life, the more you become master over the memories of your mind. The more we become masters over the memories, the more successful we will be at combating any compulsion to cling to our past.

B. Focus Forward into the Future

Another part of God's strategy to assist us in living the healed life is the strategy of focusing forward into the future that He has fashioned for our lives. This can be seen in Isaiah 43:19-20; there, God continues with His Word through the prophet Isaiah: 1*9 Watch for the new thing I am going to do. It is happening already - you can see it now! I will make a road through the wilderness and give you streams of water there. 20 Even the wild animals will honor me; jackals and ostriches will praise me when I make rivers flow in the desert to give water to my*

The Healing Experience

chosen people. You see, part of the power of God's healing experience is that it connects us to something greater in our future that can grab a hold of our focus. Living the healed life will require us to prioritize pursuits that are more powerful and promising than the pain of the past. Healing gives the indication that our destiny is greater than what damaged us; that God has a future that must be greater than our failures. The fact that God makes provisions for our healing becomes the indication that God must have a greater future for us that demands us to recover from the brokenness in our past that is keeping us bound. If we are going to live out our healing, then our focus in life must prioritize the pursuit of the future that God has designed for our lives. Regardless of the hurts that you have or may still be experiencing, regardless of how bad it was or how bad it may be, you have to absorb the truth of God's destiny that far outweighs the experiences of your history or current reality. There is a better life ahead of you. God's promises that are placed in your future will prove to be greater than the pain of your past and present experiences and the bible confirms this for us. This future that is greater than any experience of hurt in our past or even our present has its basis in biblical application. When reading 1 Corinthians 2:9 which says, *eyes have not seen nor ears heard, neither has it entered the hearts of men the things that God has **in store** for those who love Him*; and in Jeremiah 29:11 (NIV) where the bible says, *11 For I know the plans I have for you," declares the Lord, "plans to prosper you and not to harm you, plans to give you hope and a future,* it is safe to apply the principle that regardless of the current conditions of our lives, no matter how hurtful the experiences were, God has greater experiences in our future than the hurting experiences of our past. If you put this understanding in the context of healing, it becomes clear that in order for the healing experience to maintain its effectiveness in our lives, we must not only refrain from clinging to the past, but we must become intentional about connecting our energy and connecting our desire to cling to something that is greater than our past and that is the promises of a better tomorrow. To move forward from the hurt, it will often require that we have something greater than our pain to hold on to; something greater that can shake our focus free from the pain of our past or present. This is the power of the future that God has for us. Now, to assist us in shifting our focus forward, God prepares revelation of what is to come. God provides opportunities for us to experience a glimpse of the future that He has fashioned for us. Revelation allows us to have insight as it relates to what God has planned for our lives. This is why engaging in our relationship with God is so critical. Revelation often requires relationship. The more time we spend developing our relationship with God, the more likely we'll be in position to receive revelation from God. Part of the purpose of revelation is not simply a matter of receiving insight, but with that insight comes a measure of divine inspiration that will be necessary in helping us endure and transition through our tribulations. When God provides revelation, the revelation inspires us towards a destination that now demands our concentration. When God starts showing you what He has in store for you, the only way it will be accomplished or experienced is if you give it your undivided attention. Your focus is mandated to see it come into fruition in your life. And so, when healing and specifically, the maintenance of the healing experience is the goal, we have to change the direction of our focus from situation to revelation; from tribulation to destination. The healed life requires intentional and purposeful focus, not on what you went through, and not on what you're going through, but on what lies in the future. Let's go back to Isaiah's prophetic word to the people. Notice what God speaks through the prophet. God says through the prophet, **Watch** for *the new thing I am going to do. It is happening*

The Healing Experience

already - you can see *it now!* The emphasis is on Watch and see; watch for the new thing; and see that it's happening. In other words, your focus must be on what God is showing you that He is doing or is going to do in your life. The healed life mandates high value on voyage towards the vision that God verifies with revelation and confirmation. To be consistent in that voyage, we have to focus on the vision that God has revealed and confirmed for us. What I find amazing about our relationship with God is that God is always in the business of revealing Himself and His plans concerning our lives by way of His Word and His Spirit. Even when, and may be especially when life gets darkest, revelation is primed for release. Consider your experiences at the movie theaters. One of the best parts of going to a movie theater is being able to experience the previews of coming attractions. These previews are nothing more than revelation of what is to come. Notice that in the theater, the revelation or the previews aren't displayed until the room gets dark. When life gets darkened by experiences of hurt, a part of the healing experience is the display of previews of the coming attractions concerning God's purpose and plans for your life. Now, what makes revelation powerful is not simply the communication of it, but it is the visualization of it. When God gives you revelation and you have verified that it is from God, you have to internalize it until you can visualize it. What makes previews powerful is not that the communication of what is coming, but it's the visualization that is attached to it. If healing is going to be maintained in our lives, we have to position ourselves to receive revelation from God and once we receive it, we must internalize it to the degree that we begin to visualize what God is revealing. That internalization requires us to own the participation of focus. Visualizing it will push you to experience victory in it. The key to making all of this work is owning the responsibility of combating the urge to cling. When you cling to what was done to you, it blinds you from what God is doing for you. It throws your vision off. When you cling, it can result in you either ignoring insight or incorrectly interpreting the insight you have received. What ends up happening at that point is, we either reduce what God reveals as mere coincidence or we pursue it with faulty application due to incorrect interpretation. The bottom line is that we end up operating with faulty vision. One of the reasons some people can't live the healed life is simply because their vision is bad. Some people are struggling to see what God is doing because we are seeing through the filter of what they continue to cling on to; their ability to see has been influenced by the hurt that they have already seen. Because of this, they plan their lives with the watchful eye of what hurt them in their past; they strategize under the suppression of their past and present sufferings. Until there is constraint from clinging, until we cut ourselves off from clinging, it will always be a struggle to clearly see and make strides towards the future that God has for our lives. Again, while God will assist us in healing and moving forward, it is still up to us to make the necessary decisions to help us get our focus facing in the direction of His vision and revelations for our lives. We must persistently fight every thought that would try to shift our focus off of our future. This is why counseling is such a critical collaborative component of the healing experience. Many people can't get healed and can't stay healed because they aren't taking advantage of resources that can serve as effective support systems in their healing experience. Contrary to the belief of some, counseling does not categorize you as one who is crazy. This stigma that is attached to counseling has kept many in captivity to the hurts that they have experienced in life. While for every other aspect and area of our lives, we are open to professional support, our mental health is the one area that we have allowed to suffer. Unfortunately for some, counseling is an indictment against their faith, as though God is anti-counseling. We try to pray through the concerns of our mental state; we try to trust God to heal our mind and I believe that is absolutely necessary. While praying and trusting God is necessary, our relationship with God should never be seen as being competitive with the resources that are necessary to assist us in being the best version of ourselves. The same God who designed us to need ministry leaders (professionals) to ensure that we are existing as the best version of ourselves spiritually, also designed us to need medical leaders (doctors), financial leaders (economic advisors) and educational leaders (teachers) to ensure that every area of our lives is operating at the very best level and that includes our mental health. Don't allow yourself to remain a hostage to the hurt, by refusing to seek the help of professionals who could assist you in breaking free from the hurt and focusing on the greater life beyond the hurt. The more we can stay focused on pursuing the future that God is providing, the more we'll be able to stay free from the hurts that try to hold us hostage.

C. Provide Praise while making Progress

Can I be honest with you? If you are serious about experiencing the fullness of healing in your life, the journey will not be easy. You may have already discovered this while absorbing the information presented; or maybe life itself has already shown you how difficult it is to experience and maintain authentic and effective healing in your life. Healing is serious and strenuous work. If we're not careful, the grind of trying to get healed can grip us to the degree that we give up before we actually get healed. Sometimes, the process just seems and may often get too overwhelming for us to want to remain committed to it. The problem is, if we lose the commitment, we won't reach the conclusion. This is the challenge for those who are seeking to lose weight and live

The Healing Experience

healthier lifestyles. Sometimes, it is the grind of trying to lose weight that discourages people from reaching the goal of actually losing the amount of weight they had in mind. I remember when I connected with a physical trainer at a gym. One of the first things she told me is that I won't lose the weight overnight; but in order to stay committed, I would have to be intentional about celebrating the progress that I make along the way. This concept is so critical for those who want to live a healed life. The healed life, meaning the manifestation and the maintenance of healing is going to require us to learn to make praise a priority in our lives. When we engage in praise, part of what we are doing is celebrating the fact that God has helped us make progress and this act of celebrating is critical to our healing experience. When you can become consistent in praising God, you end up cultivating an internal culture that fights against the impact and imprisonment of hurt. I've discovered that a consistent life of praise will always help combat a life of pain. What praise will do is help shift your focus off of your pain and on to the God who has proven to be good in spite of your pain the God who is able to pull you out of your pain. Regardless of the hurt that you may be experiencing, if you can just push yourself to praise, your perspective will be opened to see that there is progress happening in spite of the pain that may still be there. Praise will open your eyes to see what God has done, is doing and is able to do regardless of the hurt that is trying to hold you hostage. You see, it's hard to engage in praise and simultaneously remain imprisoned to the pain of your past. One will rise above the other. That decision is on us; we must make it a priority to respond in praise especially when God performs in our lives. Praise is not simply an emotional response, but it's an essential responsibility. Praise is a response that we are responsible for because the One to whom we offer praise has and still performs at a level that deserves to receive a response of praise. Regardless of how we may

The Healing Experience

feel, we must make it a priority to push through the feeling and engage in praise because God's performances in our lives deserve it. This is what it means to make praise a priority; it means we allow nothing to get in the way of God getting the praise in response to His performance in our lives. This kind of praise has a tremendous impact on the maintenance of healing in our lives. This is how it works; when you can keep your focus on the God who is able to perform in your life, that focus should spark praise. Your praise begins to patrol the parameters of your mind in order to keep your mind guarded from the invasion of memories that would hinder you from maintaining the healing experience that God has for your life. Every time a memory shows up to enslave you or imprison you, praise immediately counters with memories and thoughts of what God has done and what God is doing. This now gives hope and confidence in what God is able and willing to do. That is why the bible reminds us to *rejoice in the Lord always and again I say rejoice* because your praise shifts your mind to the right source. When your mind is on God, that gives you peace regardless of what your past says and His peace that passes all understanding will guard your heart and your mind, but that protection of peace for your heart and your mind must flow out of the source of you rejoicing in the Lord. When you make praise a habit, praise will keep you out of the prison of your hurts. In other words, the effectiveness of the healing experience will mandate the engagement of your praise experience. The more you can have praise experiences, the more peace you will have to help you maintain the results of God's healing experience in your life. Part of living the healed life is learning not to take progress for granted. Regardless of how small the steps may be, learn to see that even small steps means that you're no longer standing in the same spot. That alone is a reason to praise and celebrate what God has done in your life. Learn to pause during the process to Praise God for any

The Healing Experience

progress made. Don't rush by progress; learn to make a big deal about the progress and a bigger deal about the God who helped you make the progress.

In closing, to be clear, the healing experience is not a "get healed quick" scheme. While God can do a quick work, while God has and can still provide immediate results, it is important to understand that both the manifestation and the maintenance of the healing experience is more often a process that is full of intense work. If you are willing to engage the process and execute the principles, I believe you will experience progress and enjoy the prize of healing throughout your life. Regardless of the hurts that you may have experienced in life, regardless of how stuck you may seem, this book was written to encourage and enlighten you in the Lord. You don't have to live your life being a hostage to your hurts. We have a healer in Father God who has strategically made healing available and accessible through the finished work of Jesus, the Christ. As a result, Earth has no sorrows that heaven can't heal. If you have been hurting, be encouraged; if you are currently going through a hurting experience, while you may genuinely feel like there is no hope beyond the hurt, I want to encourage your faith in God to believe that God has a healing experience just for you. Take advantage of the healing experience that only heaven can provide; and let me also encourage you to seek God for strong support systems that can help you not only experience healing, but can help you maintain healing in your life. Seek God to help you establish a support system (pastors, spiritual counselors, inner healing ministers, mental health professionals, and life coaches) to help you with your healing experience. Part of the reason that God had me write this book is because God has given me the responsibility of serving as a safe support system for those who heal. If you are in need of the kind of healing that will result in health and wellness for your soul, my wife

The Healing Experience

and I would love the opportunity to walk alongside you in this process and serve as your safe support system. If you would like more information, please visit us at www.kissfromheaven.life.

As you seek God for your personal healing experience, I come into agreement with your pursuit and heaven's provision of the healing experience that will result in you being healed and living healed. Excellence was my goal. My advice to you, dream you can touch the sky; then start working on a plan to make it happen.

The Healing Experience

The Healing Experience Notes:

Jeremiah 29:11

"For I know the plans I have for you, declares the Lord, plans for good and not for evil, to give you hope and a future."

PREVIOUS RELEASED BY RICARDO DORCEAN
Available on Amazon
Register for The Healing Experience Program at

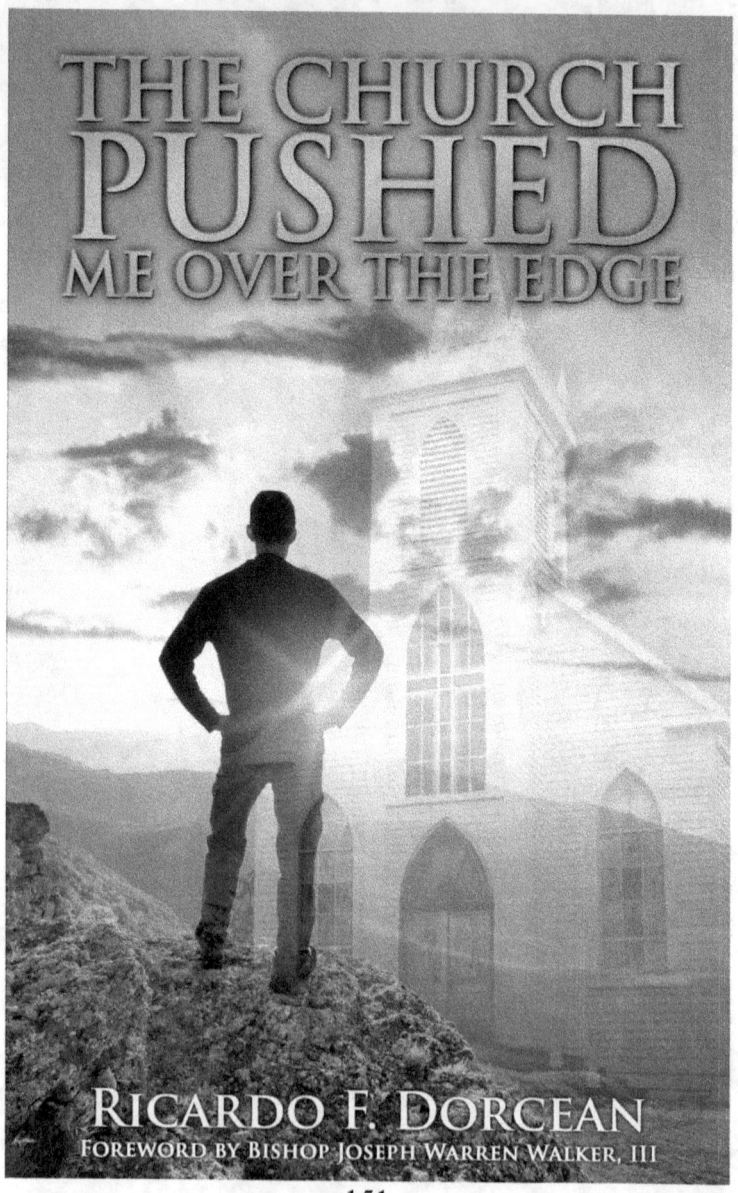

https://www.kissfromheaven.life/

www.ingramcontent.com/pod-product-compliance
Lightning Source LLC
Chambersburg PA
CBHW071851070526
44583CB00016B/1639